THE SECRET OF KNOWING

THE SCIENCE OF INTUITION

By

Laurence De Rusha

JDP Corporation

1989 19th Street #B

Boulder, CO 80302

De Rusha, Laurence, 1948-
The Secret of Knowing: The Science of Intuition
1. Intuition (Psychology)—problems, exercises 2. Intuition
(Psychology) 3. Spirituality
I. Title.
Includes bibliographic references.
ISBN 1451569777
EAN-13 9781451569773

Published by JDP Corporation
1989 19th Street #B
Boulder, CO 80302

Copy editing and text design: Angela Renkoski, akrenkoski.com

Visit our website at **www. thesecretofknowing.com**

Author's Note

This book and the stories contained herein are meant to inspire and educate the reader. No part of this book is intended as a substitute for competent medical diagnosis.

Each of the cases portrayed in this book involved people who received treatments that were specific for them and their circumstances.

Readers are cautioned and encouraged to seek the advice of competent medical practitioners who can advise how best to apply the concepts and therapies discussed in this book for their specific conditions.

This book does not replace the services of your physician, psychotherapist, or psychiatrist, and it is not meant to provide an alternative to professional medical treatment.

About the Author

Laurence De Rusha experienced a near-death, which opened his intuition and knowing. He has authored two other books: *The Roar From Within: Your Destiny Calls* and *Romancing the Divine*, a book of poetry.

Acknowledgments

I would like to thank my life partner, Marigene De Rusha, for her support, insights, and love; and my mom and dad who created my life.

Thanks also to my close friend Chuck Pettet for his advice and insights during the writing of this book and for sharing his intuitive business experiences as a top commodity trader for more than twenty years.

To Mari Davis for making the first edits to the manuscript and to Angela Renkoski for her superb editorial work in making this book readable and ready for the audience—thanks!

To all those who helped on this project, including Dr. James P. Pottenger, of LACCRS; Dr. Robert McDonald at Telos Healing Center; Charles McClendon at Gallup; Tami, Tyler, Stephen, and Kayla Collins; and all those at the Center for Spiritual Living in St. Louis, Missouri—thanks!

If you would like a safe place to discover more about the power within you, visit a Center for Spiritual Living in your area. Find one at *www.unitedcentersforspiritualliving.org/Find_A_Community/center.php*

I would also like to thank all my workshop and classroom participants for their willingness to explore the unknown, and for giving me the chance to develop my own intuitive skills, leading to this book.

Finally, I am grateful to the works of many authors and teachers who have given me insight into intuition through the years.

How to Use This Book

There is so much I wanted to include in this book but didn't because the sheer volume of information on the subject of intuition is overwhelming. I decided to take a different approach and include a fictional story at the beginning because you were more likely to choose the book because it was both entertaining and contained the non-fiction. After all, we are storytellers and love hearing a good yarn. So, yes, I began the book with the short story then moved into the non-fictional science and quasi-science of intuition. Intuition is nothing if it is not experienced. Therefore, the last section includes experiments and exercises to develop your greatest gift.

Please visit our website *www.thesecretofknowing.com* for updates, audio versions of some of the exercises, mp3 audios of workshops, and a schedule of my upcoming workshops.

CONTENTS

CONTENTS

FOREWORD

More than sixty years ago I was involved in a traffic accident. I was unconscious, barely alive, having suffered a serious head trauma. While in the ambulance, paramedics determined that I had died. They delivered my body from the hospital to the morgue, and upon arrival, the handling personnel noted movement under the covering sheet. Shortly thereafter, I was back at the hospital. Attending physicians worried that even if I regained consciousness, probable brain damage would render me permanently incapacitated.

After many doctor visits and little hope of normal functioning, my mother heard about Dr. Ernest Holmes, founder of Religious Science and Science of Mind, and his organization's orientation to spiritual healing. Although I remember nothing of the time up to my healing, I have enjoyed a marvelous career as a research scientist testing Dr. Holmes's theories.

I believe humanity is awakening to their transcendent aspect, which Dr. Holmes named our "universal mind." At some stage in our life, we might mistakenly believe in an "individual mind" and refuse to accept the possibility of a transcendent aspect being a part of our nature. There are in fact scientists who still use the words "mind" and "brain" as synonyms.

In our research and the development of Holographic Psychology/ Science of Spirit, there are three levels of reality understanding through which an individual can live his or her life. The first-reality perspective of human beings believes that learning is the result of external input from the external world and that the outside world is causing his or her problems. This level is represented by a behavioristic psychology model, producing a world that is based on cause and effect in which humans are the victims of their environment. This justifies a level of human acceptance based on outer authority control, both sacred and secular.

In second-level reality understanding, the individual believes that his or her inner world is causing his or her outer world. This presents a total reversal of the cause and effect model in which the outer causes the inner. Second level is the result of a paradigm shift in which a person's self, or ego, awakens.

This second level is researched by humanistic psychology, producing a world in which the individual is capable of becoming responsible and empowered in his or her decision-making process. In this level, the individual discovers the part neurons play in his or her programmed brain that determine behavior.

Finally, in third-level reality understanding, the individual recognizes a transcendent pre-existing wholeness. Dr. Carl Jung called this the "collective unconsciousness," and Holmes named this aspect of human nature "universal mind." It is in this transcendent reality that the "highest" level of mystical intuition operates. This level of intuition taps the pre-existing wholeness and is capable of answering questions that could scarcely be answered in a first or second reality understanding. This level is researched by transpersonal psychology, producing a world based on the inclusion of all three reality understandings.

I have been actively researching these three areas of psychology for more than fifty years. Our research validates what Larry De Rusha indicates in his book: that both true learning and healing result from the acceptance and/or actualization of a pre-existing wholeness existing within our transcendent aspect. His book is one of the best on this subject, offering a clear approach to intuition, using the psychological levels and the physiological and mystical aspects of BEING.

The Secret of Knowing is well researched and does something few books offer: it includes a fictional account of the subject, peppered with references that are followed up later in the guidebook to the scientific research into intuition and in an experiential guide, where the reader is advised to take up specific intuitive practices using the tools provided.

Intuition has been a topic for many decades but has not always been explained in scientific terms that are favorably cast or seriously explored. One of the main scientific precepts of this book is to provide an avenue for experiencing the phenomenon of intuition. This can be achieved only by repeatable processes in order to create favorable results. This book is about informing, experimenting with, and experiencing the nature of intuition.

Larry De Rusha and his marvelous wife, Marigene, have been active ministers of the Church of Religious Science (now called The Centers for Spiritual Living), teaching Science of Mind for more than twenty years.

This book provides a road map to more successful and beneficial intuition practices. I urge you to develop your greatest gifts by discovering your awesome potential awaiting actualization.

Dr. James Pottenger
President, LACCRS, Inc.
Jamul, California

— Section One —

The Secret of Knowing

The Story

PROLOGUE

Long ago, when words were pictures, a camel driver crossing his boring desert trade route to the headwaters of the Khabur River thought he could see a great tree wavering in the rolling white desert heat. This mirage felt different than others he had seen. He couldn't explain: he only knew.

For more than fifteen years he had traveled this route and each new mirage brought the questions: *Is this the one? Could this be the mirage of great treasure my father spoke about?* Now, as the minutes passed, his eyes strained toward the mirage, but it was too hard to make out through the wavering heat.

Could this be the one? kept racing through his mind, followed by *Or is this just more bored wishful thinking that often sends me out of my way?* He chided himself because this same question came up day after boring day. *Yet, why not find out?* he thought. Desperate for a better vantage, he leaned forward up and out of his saddle in an attempt to gain a better view. *I must see this.*

It wasn't enough. The driver stood atop the camel's back, clinging to the reins to maintain the edge of his balance. He could just make out a shadowy figure at the base of this distant tree. *Why not?* He jerked the reins, pointing the camel toward the apparition.

The longer strides of the camel picked up speed as the driver dropped back onto the blanket saddle. He wondered, *How far out of my way am I willing to go this time?*

As he finally approached, he was astonished to see someone clothed in a monk's robe sitting cross-legged below an outstretched branch of this great tree. There was no water, no camel, and no food in evidence. But this mirage felt very real. *Could it be?* Nervous and unsure of this apparition or himself, he stammered, "How long have you been here?"

The robed, hooded person didn't look up. The driver heard, in slow, soft tones, "Seven years. Nothing is as it appears."

The driver convinced himself he was experiencing a phantom, or could this be the mirage? It didn't make sense. *Seven years? No food? No water? It's the heat. I have been riding too long. Perhaps the last water I drank was tainted.*

Turning the camel's head to leave, he started to mount, but this strange, soft voice drew him up short. A woman's blue eyes gazed out at him through a partial veil of darkness, and she said, "I must tell you a secret as my world becomes the next."

The mystified camel driver pulled on the reins, jumping down from his half-mounted position and landing at the woman's feet.

"Knowing!" she whispered. When the word had his attention, she continued. "The secret is in the eye of the heart."

These cryptic phrases were confusing to him, and yet, somehow familiar.

His camel moved abruptly, and in the next instant, the hair prickled on the back of his neck and he became frightened. *There is nothing here. Why am I jumpy? This is just a mirage.* He cautiously turned around but didn't see anyone or anything else that would cause the animal to react. His alarmed mind was getting the best of him. *Wait; there, just behind the tree—was there movement?* He stared hard, not moving a muscle. In the next moment he felt a strange breeze on his face and knew the woman was doing all of this.

"You can't always believe the eyes in your head. You can," she paused, "the eye of your heart." He didn't understand her but felt strangely attracted to her puzzling words.

The camel driver sat down and became more and more confused at his earlier reaction and her words. Suddenly he jolted up with the intense anger that comes from embarrassment. "What a waste of time!" he said out loud.

"Woman, what are you talking about? You are sun-crazy!" he yelled. He paced back and forth in front of her. There was no response.

Finally, his curiosity overtook his anger. He stopped his pacing and sat down. She proceeded in a soft whisper to tell him all. He leaned closer and closer with each word she spoke.

"And this information is for a future generation who will know what to do with it. Have it etched," the woman insisted. Night was finally pushing the daylight across the sky. A massive rain-filled cloud quickened the darkness, and the woman hastened her story.

She finished just in time. As the ominous cloud rumbled over the driver's head, he quickly mounted his camel to leave, but a flash of light struck the tree and knocked him to the ground. A moment later, he started to come around, but he got up too fast and fell unconscious again, his head flopping back against the camel's leg.

When he awoke sometime later, the woman was gone. The tree was gone. The storm was gone. *It's this heat. I must have passed out and gone into another world.*

He pulled the camel's head toward his original route and mounted. Looking back at where this mirage unfolded, he hesitated for a moment, pulling up on the reins. He still felt strange and haunted by this strong image of the woman, her blue eyes, odd monk's robe, and the mysterious secret. He tried to shake it off.

He smiled, ready to leave, knowing how crazy he must be to even think about any of this. Something on the ground caught his eye. *There, next to where my head must have hit,* he thought. He dismounted and picked up a small pouch with writing on it and something inside.

***

That evening the camel driver made his way to the small village of Ra's al-Ayn. It was an uncomfortable, humid evening. But that wasn't what bothered him. His mind was racing, and he was unable to settle down. His uneasy feeling caused him to trust no one.

He thought some wine would calm his mind, and he found a dimly lit inn near the edge of the village. He tied his camel near the entrance, pushed aside the curtain door, and walked in. As he passed the barkeeper headed for one of the empty tables in the back corner, he called out, "Wine." The man behind the counter pulled out a clay carafe and filled it with wine.

Putting the carafe on the table, the barkeep waited for payment. The camel driver barely noticed as he stared at the small pouch he had found. The barkeep tapped him on the shoulder and the driver placed a coin on the table. He fought the unreal images of what had happened earlier in the desert that now repeatedly flashed in his mind. *Was it real? How could she sit like that for seven years?* The questions circled with the images in his timeless haze. The loud noise and laughter of the men around him brought him out of his trance. His mind raced: *They are staring at me. Somehow, they know. I must have drunk too much. Was I talking out loud?*

He felt crazy with this secret burned in his mind. The questions started again. *Was the woman a priestess? Surely it was a curse?* That would explain it. His mind was now frantic, and he desperately wanted out of his own skin. *I have to tell someone this secret so I can let it go and be done with it.*

He walked his camel down the narrow main street to a holy man's home just outside the village. Upon arriving, he asked a monk sitting in front of the dwelling for help in scribing his story. The uninterested monk—smart, fast, and young—did not look up from his work until the driver whispered, "I have the Secret of Knowing."

The monk leapt up and grabbed the driver's elbow, towing him through the dark cavernous hallway and down into a room bright from what seemed like hundreds of candles. The light hurt the driver's eyes as he gazed upon hundreds of clay tablets, some stacked from floor to wooden ceiling beam.

The monk studied the camel driver for a moment, thinking. *How could this be?* Having heard rumors of this secret from his master, he was suspicious that a disheveled camel driver would possess such a powerful thing. "What proof do you have of this secret?" he asked.

The camel driver brought out the pouch. "The only evidence of this strange event is this," he said, dropping the pouch in the monk's lap. "The woman said to etch the secret and hide it and the pouch for a future generation."

The camel driver continued his story. All the while, the monk was carefully listening until he finally asked in an astonished tone, "Where did you get this? Who is this woman? Why you?" The monk knew this story would also be troublesome to his master because of its power.

After the camel driver was well on his way, the monk started etching. Knowing the trouble he would face from his master if this power were discovered by others, he decided the safest thing was to hide the words and pouch. Quickly, he finished etching four flat pieces of clay and laid them out on a table. At their base, he placed the pouch from the driver and covered it with soft clay. Then he fashioned the four inscribed pieces into a jar, sealing and smoothing the edges until they were seamless. He set the jar in the darkest corner of the room to dry and harden then quickly left.

The jar, pouch, and secret disappeared into history.

THE DESERT

Archeologist and former Cairo Museum director Taher Mustafa had experienced many eventful years in his profession. His discovery in 1945 of the seventy-three original Greek gospels, never released to the public, highlighted his early career. He felt that this recent find would, without doubt, eclipse all others and be his crowning achievement. Yet, nothing had prepared him for the mind-numbing fate about to befall him.

The sweat in his eyes was a mixture of heat and nerves. The camels lumbered across the hot desert of Syria, equipment lashed to their backs, the late summer heat turning everything into branding irons.

A moving dot coming from beyond the distant mountain backdrop caught his eye. He reached for the pair of binoculars dangling at the end of a black strap from the saddle. "Damn," he yelled, dropping them. "Bloody hot thing!" As the dot became larger, the outline of a helicopter traveling over the dunes toward Mustafa became clearer.

"What the … ?" Mustafa said, jerking the camels to a stop. Another tug on the reins and the camels settled to the ground as he slid off the lead.

A tan-and-khaki-painted chopper hovered close enough to blast a blinding, stinging spray of sand at him and his camels. He covered his eyes while peeking at this oddity. *That's crazy. What the bloody hell is going on?*

The well-worn chopper had no other markings except the visible desert camouflage colors. When the doors slid open, three men dressed in black uniforms and armed with rifles slung over their shoulders jumped to the desert floor and moved quickly toward Mustafa.

"Dr. Mustafa?" one of them yelled, speaking in a German accent.

The archeologist was bewildered. "How did you … "

"Get your satellite phone, Doctor," shouted one of the men above the noise of the helicopter.

"What? I'm sorry? Is something wrong? How did you know my name?"

One of the men pulled his rifle off his shoulder, flipping it around to grab the trigger. "Now, you idiot. Now!" Mustafa pulled the phone from his saddle pack strapped to the lead camel.

"Place a call to this number and read this message word for word."

The man handed him a torn piece of yellow paper. Mustafa recognized his museum department's laboratory phone number. *Somebody knows,* he thought.

One of the men became more aggressive and pointed his rifle at Mustafa. "Now. Call now!"

Out of the corner of his eye Mustafa saw the third man maneuvering to his side. He felt his own voice vibrate with fear as he spoke. When Mustafa finished reading, the man stuck a needle in his neck. Instantly his body crumpled to the hot sand.

Two of the men placed his lifeless body in the chopper, and it flew north, far off Mustafa's planned route and away from his camel caravan. There the chopper hovered again, the door opened, and Mustafa's inert body and empty water bottles were pushed out. If and when anyone found him, it would look as if he had been lost, run out of water, and died.

The chopper climbed and turned, heading toward the Cairo Museum. The men seemed pleased with their work. As they flew over the Syrian Desert, the men started buzzing about an ancient story of a mirage that, if found, would reveal a treasure. They continued laughing and chatting while a fourth man in black, Kakus Ramey, sat quietly in stony silence across from them.

"The camel drivers around here love this story," one of them said.

The helicopter landed on the museum's roof and Ramey jumped out. "Shut up and follow me."

THE PROFESSOR

Ubaid was worried about the strange call he had received several hours earlier from Dr. Mustafa. He pulled the 5,000-year-old pottery jar from the vault while replaying the call. "Open the vault and remove the pottery jar marked T77. It has a papyrus pouch in it. Place it on the lab counter. Wait for your contact, a man dressed in black. He will pick it up and leave. Don't talk to anyone about this call or your family will … "

"Morning, Professor," Amir said from his post at the staff entrance, without looking up from his newspaper. Amir didn't need to see who was passing by; he knew the regulars. With his morning coffee in one hand and newspaper in the other, he liked to pretend he was on the sidewalk of a Paris café with friends.

Jean-François Laurence headed through the door, passing in silence as he always did. The professor walked down the stairs to his laboratory, passing the rack of white smocks near the lab door. As a self-proclaimed "adventurous" archeologist, he never wore the traditional white laboratory smock. Instead, he liked to project—unlike his actual feelings of fear and failure—an image born from the strong, daring, self-confident character of Indiana Jones.

Although a slight variation from Indy's getup, his safari outfit sported a phony university insignia and an award patch like billboards on the sleeve. Out of his plastic pocket protector, the icon of status among archeologists, he pulled his security card. He swiped it and a small red light on the security reader flashed. The door remained locked. "Always something," he said out loud. He swiped the card again, and the lab building door unlocked.

He made his way to his laboratory. Once inside the small confines, he noticed that the print of de Kooning's *Woman III* that Director Mustafa had given him was crooked. Straightening it, Jean-François smiled slightly at the thought of the many long talks he and Mustafa had had about this painting.

The professor also noticed his book manuscript sitting on one of the stools. He walked over and picked it up, tossing it onto the counter in disgust. He sat hard on the wooden stool, pulling his legs up and propping them on the stool's leg bars.

He sighed, muttering, "Boring. Just so damn boring. Katie and I should head back to Lindenwood where at least somebody knows who I am." He was resigned to being a big fish in his small university pond.

In Cairo to finish his overdue book on the ancient Eshnunna codex, but secretly hoping for a shocking breakthrough that would put him on the cover of *TIME* magazine, he felt nothing but boredom.

It takes too much research and it's so much writing, and where the Jesus is the excitement? I need to change the flight reservation and leave this week, he thought.

Looking at the phone on his desk, he pulled his feet from the stool and started to move. Then he noticed one of the museum's pottery jar relics left out on the nearby table. *Damn! Don't they realize how delicate these are, for God's sake?*

His angry thoughts were part of an overall frustration lately. He didn't want to go home again without being famous. But there were other frustrations, like the sloppy operation of the museum ever since the new director had taken over.

To Jean-François's amazement, Mustafa had been demoted just two weeks ago and immediately assigned to an artifact hunt in the Syrian Desert. *Alone! He must have really screwed up—like the idiot who left this jar out.*

He grabbed a pair of latex gloves from the box on his desk, pulling them on as he walked over to pick up the clay jar. *Hmm. Old papyrus writings were probably housed in it for thousands of years. I bet Ubaid cracked this pot and left it.* He snapped on one of the gloves and gripped the jar. *The vault was only ten feet away, the lazy morons.*

He put his arm inside the jar to keep it stabilized but somehow lost control of it. Suddenly the jar was rolling. Quickly he grabbed it with his other hand. His hand inside the jar grazed the inside wall, and he instantly recognized the clay was etched.

Excited by the possibilities, he found the lab's small digital camera in his desk drawer and lowered it into the jar with one of his gloved hands. He moved the camera slowly to avoid hitting the delicate clay walls and snapped several pictures.

I know all these pots. None are etched. He pulled the camera out of the jar and peeked at the camera's preview screen. He was stunned.

He lowered the camera into the jar again but, unsettled by what he saw, he lost his grip. The camera dropped several inches, stopping with a dull thud. *That should have made a cracking sound, not a muted sound.*

Jean-François raised the jar above his head, looking at the outside bottom for cracks. At the same time, his gaze was drawn through his raised, outstretched arms to someone dressed in black watching him through the lab door window. But his concern was for the jar, and he moved his attention back to what he was doing. *No cracks? Must have broken inside.* He slid his arm into the jar with one hand, feeling around the base.

There! Something's there in the base. It's not broken clay. It's loose. Dizzy with excitement, he was startled by Ubaid coming out of the bathroom.

"Let me put that back, Professor!" Ubaid said, panicking. "It's just one of the containers from the 1930 Eshnunna site. I forgot to put it back!"

Ubaid ran toward the professor, who was still holding the pottery jar. Ubaid stretched out his hands, motioning for the professor to give the jar to him.

"Why are you here, Professor? Didn't the new director tell you to stay away for a week? Aren't you supposed to be on holiday? What are you doing with the jar?"

Jean-François stared at Ubaid in surprise, then began telling him what had just happened. The professor brought the digital camera out of the jar and pushed the button for the preview screen to light up. They were looking at the pictures on the small preview screen when Ubaid became more agitated as he searched through the lab door window for the contact Mustafa had mentioned.

Jean-François gasped. "This appears to be a language older than even the Sumerians' language!" He caught himself before he blurted anything about the pouch he had found at the bottom of the jar, testing to see what Ubaid might know.

Ubaid's face turned a cold ash color. "This is part of the Tell Halaf find, not Eshnunna," the professor said. When Ubaid didn't respond, the professor turned. Ubaid was gone. Movement outside the lab door window caught Jean-François's eye, and he saw a fidgety Ubaid wildly talking with the man in black.

That's the guy I saw just a few minutes ago, Jean-François thought.

The professor moved closer to the lab door where a muffled conversation was leaking through. He reacted. "Ubaid! Ubaid! We can't let anyone know until we check the catalog and registry on this jar."

The lab door partially opened as Ubaid stuck his head in. "Professor? The new director demands you wait for him to come down." His speech betrayed a deep fear.

"Ubaid! Don't you remember all the infighting that kept the Nag Hammadi discovery from being publicized for twenty-eight years?" Jean-François shot back. "And how do you explain Dr. Mustafa's find of those Greek gospels unreleased to the public?"

Ubaid walked through the door toward the professor while the man in black walked the other way. "The Nag Hammadi would still be under lock and key in a vault if it wasn't for one professor's need of assistance in interpreting the language," Jean-François continued. "He took pictures and sent them out to colleagues. But Mustafa's gospel find is still in the vault after fifty years because of politics."

Ubaid wasn't listening. He began to speak over the professor's voice. "You have to put the jar back and you have to stay in here," Ubaid demanded. His voice was a strange combination of intimidation and nervousness. This tall, athletic-looking Egyptian was frustrated, mystified, and angry, trying to obey his old boss's orders as well as the man in black's new threats.

Jean-François could feel his own anger rise inside. He was torn between another hush-hush find and political football and his intense desire to make this the path to his fame. Instead of exploding, however, he walked over to Ubaid with the pottery jar and coolly handed it to him. "I would be careful, Ubaid! Put this and the piece inside back in the archive vault before something happens to them. And don't forget," he said, pointing to the box of gloves. Ubaid ran for the latex gloves, knowing he had no choice; he had to put the jar away for the moment, but then he needed to get it to the man in black soon so nothing would happen to him or his family.

As Ubaid entered the vault, his attention was on the inside of the jar. Mustafa and the man in black had mentioned a pouch. But there was no pouch inside the bottom of the jar—all he could feel were broken clay shards. He froze. *I am dead.*

The professor spun around, regretting having shown Ubaid the pictures, but he had bigger concerns. He headed for the lab counter, snagging the camera and his brown lunch bag. He knew he had to move quickly. *This is a find everyone will try to claim and some would try to hide.*

As Jean-François bounded up the stairs leading to the staff entrance, the elevator door on the lab floor below opened, and the voice of the new museum director echoed up the stairs. Jean-François peered through the handrails of the stairway. The mystery man in black was excitedly looking around while mumbling a response to the director. Then they were both quiet, as if listening for him.

Jean-François's body froze. But he couldn't stop his breath. Climbing the stairs had winded him, and try as he might not to, he had to keep breathing. His mind kept saying, *run, run.*

He heard what sounded like a shot and jumped.

Did they shoot Ubaid? His mind reeled, and he questioned what he heard as he continued his sprint up the stairs. The sound of the door slamming shut below him made Jean-François go faster.

Breathing hard, he made himself slow to a walk past Amir at the staff entrance. He turned his hip to press the long flat bar to open the door. He heard Amir say, "What's all the excitement, Professor?"

He was racking his brain for an answer, wondering if there was some way Amir knew he was leaving with the camera. *The director might have called him.* "Anniversary, right? Isn't your wife here this time?" Amir offered.

The professor instinctively responded, "And I forgot!" as he pushed quickly on the bar and the door sprung open.

FLIGHT

Seventeen minutes later the professor arrived at his temporary residence on Youssif Abas near the Cairo Stadium. Occasionally, the museum provided housing for him when he was part of a larger government-sponsored expedition. This time he had found his own place because he was working on his book, and he wanted Katie here because it was to be an extended stay.

They will have some trouble finding me, as I keep forgetting to register this place with the curator's office, he thought.

In his worry about the museum's security team, he rushed and nearly fell through the front door of the apartment, tripping on the Oriental doormat, the one Katie brought wherever they went. The self-closing door slammed behind him and pushed him straight toward the kitchen, where he nearly crushed the brown bag with the camera in it. "Jesus Christ."

I'll put the camera in the pantry drawer. Then he changed his mind and put it back into the lunch bag and placed the bag in the garbage can, a less likely place for the camera.

The walls of the large kitchen were covered with the candid photos of couples kissing that Katie was constantly taking and collecting. Katie sat on a barstool at the kitchen peninsula counter sipping a Diet Coke, one of the few she had found anywhere in the city.

Katie Lange was a sociologist at Washington University in St. Louis and, like her husband, had a flair that was definitely more than academic. She was an attractive thirty-something; at the moment she was wearing a khaki-colored, sleeveless calf-length dress with rhinestone studs bordering the scoop neck, highlighting her well-defined arms and shoulders, not to mention her newly acquired bust. Her gold sandals, covered by faceted glass jewels and metallic gold trim, topped off the look. A bit ostentatious, but she didn't care. Since she had decided to take six months off and come with Jean-François to Egypt, she certainly wasn't going to wear business suits.

She turned from the miniature TV, her light brown hair, barely fashioned, swirling around her face. *No one in this country understands hair,* she thought. Since being called a geek in high school, she had learned exactly how to handle her hair to impress people with her sexy but smart locks. As her hair cleared her deep blue eyes, she caught the professor's anxious facial expression. "Jerry? What's wrong?" she said without thinking.

His name was not really Jean-François Laurence, but he had legally changed it because the name had a bold and daring sound to it. Jerry Smith hardly fit his desired image. Katie loved this showman part of him—Indiana Jones or bad boy meets professor—and her quixotic archeologist was tall and lean, with a frame made for everything but a swimsuit.

He didn't answer. She set the cola can on *The Da Vinci Code* book she had started reading a few hours earlier.

"And I didn't even have to call you, honey," she said, knowing how often she had to phone him and suggest he stop work and spend some time with her. She reached toward him. "Where is my kiss … uh … hug?" She turned to follow him as he walked around the counter.

He didn't hear her. He was making every effort to impose order on his racing mind. He liked order. He was always organized and meticulous. Being a professor of archaeology required attention to detail and order—and friends.

"I called Shankara in Berkeley," he said, nervously. "Ah … just a few minutes ago."

Shankara Jones was a professor of ancient languages, and she, Jean-François, and an art dealer had spent several summers searching for tombs and caves in Egypt's deserts. Strange bedfellows perhaps, Jean-François sometimes thought, but all of them were explorers, even the art dealer.

"Shankara was so quiet I'm not sure she believed me about the pictures." Jean-François's tone was very serious. He could hear his words flowing out of his mouth, but his mind was thinking about booking a flight and getting to the airport.

Katie looked at him, waiting for a comment on their anniversary or at least the beginning of the story. When it was apparent she was getting neither one, she muttered under her breath, "What picture?"

"Pictures!" Jean-François exploded. "Pictures!!"

His anger summoned memories of the way her father could erupt and yell. She sat in the heavy silence, feeling something pushing up from her stomach to her chest as she slipped into that old familiar feeling of fear. Growing up, her father was a raging alcoholic and exploded in much the same way as Jean-François. And when the balloon of her dad's anger had popped, Katie knew she had to keep track of all the pieces or there would be nasty consequences. Although Jean-François's anger wasn't as frequent or violent, she sometimes felt she had married her father. She stared intently at him while forcing herself to breathe.

Finally Jean-François noticed the stricken look on Katie's face and pushed himself to calm down and continue. "You're right. Yes, sorry, I, I bet they already know. We have to get the hell out of here to the airport. ... We need to leave, Katie, ... now!"

"Jerry," she caught herself again using his given name. These were the kind of mistakes that caused trouble. Her mind raced almost in sync with his. *Jean-François isn't making much sense.* Thoughts were pouring through her mind, and she felt the fear of being in a foreign country and not knowing what to do if her husband had gone crazy. *What if it was something more?*

He was visibly trembling and moving fast. Katie knew this meant he was in trouble. From her father's rampages, she also knew what to do next: stay out of the way and pick up the pieces afterward.

Jean-François was intent on his internal conversation but finally took notice of Katie. "Katie, I found ... ." He paused, not sure how to explain what had happened, then he began running up the stairs to pack. His mind flashed back to sprinting up the stairs at the lab and the sound of a shot, and the same anxiety washed over him. He told Katie of the strange events, leaving out some of the more troublesome details.

Katie stopped halfway up the stairs. A corner of her book on the kitchen counter caught her attention. *This is sounding like that Da Vinci Code.* She noted that beads of sweat had formed on the corner from the Diet Coke, staining the cover of the hardback even as the heat caused the moisture to evaporate instantly.

Jean-François wiped the sweat from his forehead, saying, "I told Shankara we would fly to California to see her. But I think we should fly through St. Louis and get a separate airline ticket to California. That way it will make the museum security, who will quickly trace us, think we went back to the university. Hopefully, it will stall them. We should arrive in eighteen hours. I'll call Shankara again and let her know."

Katie walked from the closet to the bed as Jean-François hesitantly said, "They'll be alarmed, Katie. Because this is the first find that uses a cuneiform language inscribed inside a Tell Halaf clay jar. But this is also the only known relic from …"

"How did a pottery jar survive 5,000 years?" she asked, grabbing her clothes from the drawer.

"This one was fired. Even though they didn't fire their pottery back then, they placed the soft clay pots or tablets on shelves so they would air-dry. They didn't know about fire making the clay stronger. It's why we have lost so many artifacts from that period."

He continued explaining, his mind clearing now that he had a plan. "Over the millennia, treasure hunters looted the old sites. They would leave the worthless jars and tablets because they couldn't sell them. The ironic thing is that when they tried to cover their tracks by setting fire to holy sites, such as a monastery, they inadvertently fired the clay, making it stronger."

"How could the museum team screw up so much on this jar?" she said.

"No, I don't feel they screwed up. I think I foolishly stumbled into something bigger going on," Jean-François said. "The way Ubaid and this mysterious man in black reacted leads me to believe someone already knew about the importance of this jar and was planning something."

That Ubaid might be dead means there was a crime, but why commit a crime unless there is something else illegal—and dangerous—happening? He kept this thought to himself.

THE LAB

"I don't want to keep harping on this point, but are you sure this is a good idea, Jean-François? Coming to San Francisco? Fleeing Egypt without telling anyone? Did you call Mustafa?" Katie often asked many questions in rapid succession, not really looking for an answer.

Jean-François answered in his usual way, which was to just think out loud and not try to address any specific question of hers. "What else can I do? I don't trust anyone. We have to find a safe place to download and examine the pictures with someone more familiar with this language."

They drove across the Oakland Bay Bridge headed for Shankara's lab on the UC-Berkeley campus. The mid-morning sky was bright and clear, but the fog blanketed the Golden Gate Bridge, leaving only the top of the towers eerily exposed.

The four-cylinder rented car slowed appreciably as it climbed the Oakland Hills toward campus. "But the museum people you spoke of? Well, surely they are after you, you know." She shrugged. "Surely they already know where we … " Fear was pulling her mind. "Your running and all of it. When they find us, what then?"

He ignored the question, raising her suspicions.

Jean-François drove up to Shankara's lab building. They could see the Berkeley campus wandering for acres, with its labs and classroom buildings jutting from groves of trees here and there.

"There! Let's stay there." Katie pointed to the sprawling white Claremont Resort nestled in the hills. "Then we can return the car and we're safe. We can walk from there to the lab, right?" She waited for her husband's reply.

Katie was confident in her own mind that the resort would be the last place they would look. It was always the cheap motels the cops searched first, according to the *Perry Mason* shows she used to watch. The bad guys seemed to always think no one looks there.

As a child she would sip on a cola and watch *Perry Mason* on their TV in the motel room—home—until Dad came. Then she would chat about school and his day until the bottle came out. A drink or two later, she would sneak out and head to Room 70. Her friend was a young woman who lived in the room, worked nights, and knew Katie's plight. She gave her a key for when she needed it.

Jean-François interrupted her memories. "You're right. I'll bet they wouldn't look for us in a resort."

Katie came out of the flashback wondering why she had thought about the cops. "This wasn't some crime, was it? Was it, Jean-François?" The stress of the recent events and the strain of the long hours of travel were evident in her tone.

He didn't want to answer her, so he motioned her to look at the city overlooking the bay. He had indeed stolen the pouch from the jar, wanting to become famous for the discovery. He couldn't be absolutely sure about what had happened to Ubaid, but he knew, at the very least, the fact that he had taken antiquities out of Egypt meant he had committed a crime.

***

"I have always wanted to stay in this resort," Jean-François quipped as he saw Shankara enter the resort lobby. He did a double take of her body. *Fifteen years … she looks great.* He realized something was troubling her, though, when he looked into her eyes. Her hazel eyes had always been a tell-tale sign. She was anxious and he could now feel it. "Shankara! I love this place," he said, attempting small talk. Shankara's zero response was confirmation something was very wrong.

"Professor Laurence, why stay in a resort right next to your friend's lab?" A tall hefty man dressed in black growled and moved into Jean-François's line of vision from one of the foyer alcoves.

The man's eyes were trained on the professor, looking for any sign he might run. "What trouble you must be in for the department to classify this as high priority! Why is it nowadays you professors seem to be making the news with all the mystery stuff?"

Who is this guy? How did they know we were here so fast? Someone must have followed us from Cairo. In a moment of pure shock Jean-François realized, *Oh, my God. This is the guy at the museum lab!*

Shankara nervously introduced Ramey as a special Egyptian diplomatic envoy. "Move outside," he said, not asking but demanding. This guy's act of being a special diplomatic envoy didn't fool Jean-François. Other than being dressed in all black, he looked like a Delta Force or black ops soldier ready to deal with or create trouble. *He must be the one who shot Ubaid!*

Katie had been handling the hotel's check-in process when Ramey appeared. When she turned back a few moments later, Ramey, Shankara, and Jean-François were walking out the double glass doors to the covered entry. Katie wondered why Jean-François didn't turn and wink at her as he always did. Trying to shrug off some old feelings, she finished the check-in form. While she was signing it, she thought about who the guy holding Jean-François's arm might be.

She walked outside to join them. The wind blowing through the covered entrance caused Katie to move her arm to her face to hold her hair from wildly circling her head. Wisps of hair stung her large blue eyes as she tried to identify the other guy.

"Is this your wife, Professor? Come, come. Let's all head over there."

A black Mercedes pulled under the canopy. *This was certainly not the police,* Jean-François thought. It wasn't the usual black luxury Town Car from the government motor pool either.

A man opened the passenger side door and got out, standing about ten feet from Jean-François. The driver stood next to the door of the Mercedes. Both men were tall, stout, and muscular, and dressed in black. They had the ruthless faces of mercenaries.

"Professor Jean-François? You think you could get away with this?"

Ramey stopped, his attitude abruptly changing to anger. "We need this to be quick and easy. Give us the camera and my German friends will leave you alone or ... ." He motioned to the men at the car and one of them grabbed Katie. "Understand?"

Jean-François struggled to pull the digital camera from his coat pocket. Just as he was about to hand it to Ramey, his mind flashed from Katie to Ubaid. *Guys like this can't always win and this discovery is too important,* he thought.

He needed to stall them and somehow get the memory card out of the camera quickly. He flashed through ideas.

"Hey, wait. How do I know you aren't going to kill all of us?" he said, pulling the camera back from Ramey's hand and putting it behind him. He backed into Shankara, who understood immediately.

"If I make a scene right here, hotel security will come running," Jean-François said, mainly to divert attention from Shankara. But Ramey could sense something was happening, could feel his bounty slipping away.

"Give me the damn camera. Give it to me and you can all go. But more stalling and I'll ... ." He motioned, moving his chin to the man holding Katie, who pulled her hair, causing her head to snap back.

As if on cue, the wind blew thick swirls of dust across the driveway right into Ramey's eyes. He lowered his head, blinking furiously. Jean-François was pressing his luck he knew, but he asked, "Ramey, how much are you willing to pay?"

Shankara pressed her tall well-proportioned body against Jean-François, the tiny camera passing back from Shankara before anyone knew she had taken the memory card. Ramey, still brushing his eyes, yelled, "What the hell is going on?"

The commotion agitated the Mercedes driver, who was standing with his arms perched on the roof, ready for the next move. The professor palmed the camera and handed it to Ramey.

"Good!" In his mind, Ramey felt relief. It had been easier than he figured.

"I knew you would be smart about this." He fumbled with the camera.

"Hey, be careful with that!" the professor barked as another distraction.

"I will also take that pouch, Professor," Ramey said. Until now, Jean-François wasn't sure if Ramey knew about the pouch. His detailed mind, however, realized on the flight to San Francisco that this might happen. Having just enough time while waiting for the rental car, he had wrapped up some apple seeds from Katie's in-flight snack in a souvenir papyrus pouch he had picked up at the Cairo airport, originally intending to use it to wrap Katie's "I'm sorry" gift. There was no time to buy it at the museum after he realized he needed it.

He stretched out his arm and handed the pouch over to Ramey. The other man let Katie go, and she raised her hand as if to hit the guy. He smirked at her, showing his contempt. "It's all right, Katie," Jean-François said, pulling her into him.

***

An hour later, Shankara and Katie sat opposite Jean-François in Shankara's lab. Shankara made coffee and took a sip. "This is harsh. Wow! I still can't make good coffee or cook."

Jean-François and Shankara used to be lovers. They had met in college and kept in contact, and when he found an art dealer who would pay for his artifact hunts, he called Shankara to go with them. Her ancient language skills and highly visible professorship at a major university made the art dealer feel more secure about funding them.

Although Shankara's father named her after his favorite East Indian seventh-century philosopher, the deserts of the Middle East were as close as she had come to seeing India.

The trips in the desert the three of them made were long, sometimes two to three weeks. There was continued closeness between Jean-François and Shankara, and the evenings spent under the desert sky were conducive to many conversations and passionate feelings. Perhaps it was their similar tough childhoods that sparked their attraction and lead to their rough but playful sex during those many trips over the years.

Katie knew about their college connection, and she suspected something more but never wanted to expose herself to more pain by asking Jean-François. And as he never spoke of her anymore, it was an easy way to avoid the subject. Now she had no choice; it was in her face. The energy between Shankara and Jean-François was palpable. Katie swallowed hard, knowing this wasn't the time for confrontation.

Jean-François was still looking around the lab. White chalk formulas and scribbles were all over the blackboards, and in the lower left corner was a telephone number with a country code prefix for Cairo and one of the museum's extensions. Jean-François shook his head back and forth, trying to quell a weird desire to laugh and cry at the same time.

Jean-François had a hunch there was a connection between Ramey and Shankara, but he tried to dismiss it. He wasn't completely sure, but his turning stomach and sinking feeling felt like confirmation of jealousy.

He sighed. "Let's look at the photos now!" He knew Shankara was one of only a few people who could decipher the codex in the pictures. "Too bad we can't wait for the prints of the pictures, Shankara. It would be easier than this small screen on the camera."

Shankara didn't seem to feel any urgency. "What's going on, Jean-François? And what was the pouch you handed to them?"

Jean-François answered, "Don't you know?" He showed her one of the pictures on the camera screen, pointing to the left. "This is the pouch—and look at the symbols. What's this symbol? See, here?"

"It's a symbol of approval. You know, like a special stamp from the ruler."

"What about this? Is this some prophecy? What about this one?"

She was looking at strange characters in a pose on the next picture and said, "Might be instructions on how to be some type of shaman? Something about accessing spirits." Shankara smiled. "I will tell you, it doesn't make me feel better to know Sylvia or what's-her-name, the psychic, probably wrote this in a past life and we almost got killed for it." She laughed nervously at her own poor humor.

A moment later Shankara said, "So you didn't answer me when I asked what you'd passed to Ramey."

"We need to leave," Jean-François said curtly. "Your lab is too risky. I know Ramey and his thugs will be back when they discover the memory card is missing, and this will be the first place they look."

***

They exited the lab building in a hurry and headed for the nearby public area where they could blend in with the college students. They walked to a street café down the road. On the way Jean-François commented that prophets and prophecy 5,000 years ago were held in very high regard. Most of the Old Testament and Talmud were prophecy. "Maybe this is the secret of those prophecies!"

"It doesn't make sense, Shankara," Katie said, puzzled, trying to view the digital pictures on the small camera. She jostled for a better view as they walked. "Why didn't they kill us?"

Katie continued, "Shankara, do they want something else? I still don't know what this is about." Shankara said nothing but turned to look at Katie, feeling herself at the last moment wanting to look away, hoping Katie wouldn't detect her involvement with Jean-François.

As they sat outside at the café, Jean-François saw something in the ancient pictographic words visible in the digital picture. He asked Shankara, "Do you think this is related to the Zero Point Field that Professor Putoff at Stanford is working on? And if this is an ancient method of tapping some kind of all-knowing field then ... " He didn't finish. "I need the restroom."

Shankara pointed toward the back of the shop.

He took a drink of Shankara's coffee he had brought along. "You were right. This is not good. What is this, Egyptian coffee?" He tossed it in the trash can as he headed for the restroom, pausing long enough to watch Shankara for any reaction. When none came, he asked, "Hey, Shankara? How do you know Ramey and when did he show up at the resort?"

"I don't know him. He just burst into my office about fifteen minutes before you called to say you were heading to the resort. One of his guys grabbed me and we headed over," Shankara said.

Jean-François stood at the urinal feeling angry as he recalled his earlier suspicion about Shankara. *Was the telephone number on the blackboard, the Cairo lab phone, Mustafa's extension? These uncertainties are hell. I don't feel good about being here. We have to get out of here.*

As he walked back toward the table, he said to Katie, "We need to head for the airport and get to Chicago." He noticed Shankara's look of surprise and her quick response.

"Should I get copies of the pictures?"

He didn't reply, knowing that he wanted to study the pictures for himself—and he was still unsure of her.

***

Detective Darcy was one of those police detectives who spent too much time worrying about their cases: gray, grouchy, and cynical. He didn't like suits or ties and usually wore Dockers and long-sleeve shirts. He had been notified by his superiors that Nike running shoes were inappropriate attire, but with twenty-eight years on the force, his record overruled their concerns.

This 50-year-old former beat cop had not clawed his way to the top detective spot. Rather, he outsmarted his competitors. Yet, after all these years he realized that his competitive nature had cost him many friends and three wives. Now he was up for retirement in just six months, and he had two prime motivators: don't die, and go out solving a high-profile case.

When the call was put through to him from a well-known Berkeley professor with international connections, he thought, *This is the one!*

Darcy arrived at Shankara's lab about twenty minutes after the call. He was upset both about being called three hours after Professor Laurence had left and by Ramey's questions.

"Detective, how did you get involved? The government didn't request any help," Ramey asked, still posing as a diplomatic envoy. "What is your connection?"

"Ramey. Is that right?" Cynicism, Darcy's stock-in-trade, served him well with guys like Ramey. Pushing back, he said, "Ah-ha, chief or envoy? How is it that when you can't get your guy, the pros have to do the real work? Never mind, don't answer."

"Yes, the name is Ramey, Kakus Ramey, Detective! It was the wind and that conniving professor who wasn't supposed to muck things up in the first place. But now we have another problem." Ramey was getting more upset as he spoke. "Jean-François has had time to view, copy, and understand the damn pictures."

"Where is he?" said the detective.

Ramey pointed menacingly to Shankara. She had called the detective because her friend was in more trouble than he could imagine, and it was getting too complex for her to deal with. "Detective, the professor left on a flight to Chicago about three hours ago.

***

The photos they'd picked up before leaving San Francisco were sitting between Jean-François and Katie. "When we land in St. Louis," Jean-François said, "Chester, my student assistant, will pick us up. I told him very little. Just that we were completing my book in Egypt and needed to return early, that kind of thing."

"Do you really think this information is that big a deal?"

"Katie, this could change the basic premise of what we know about the mind and how it works!" His thoughts were jumping around. "We'll talk about that later. On a more practical level, the people chasing us were not offering money to get any of this back, remember? They were confused it seemed to me. They might have moved in on us before they understood what was going on. That makes this unique, and it makes me wonder what they know or don't know. I think their strategy was two-pronged: One, if they got everything, they could disclaim any existence of anything, and two, they will continue trailing us in case they need to quiet us later."

"Wow." The impact was just hitting Katie. "But why? What makes this find so important?"

"There is something else, Katie, something about the Garden of Eden." Jean-François was interrupted as the plane touched down.

COSTA RICA

Jean-François stared at the toothpaste that had sat open on the sink in the St. Louis condo for the entire time they were in Egypt. He rinsed his mouth instead and was about to step into the shower when he heard his cell phone ringing. He turned toward the bathroom door. "Katie, can you get that?"

A moment later the bathroom door opened, and Katie looked around the edge at Jean-François. "Said his name was Clive. Some old friend of yours." They exchanged places. She stepped into the bathroom and stood in her cotton nightgown, hair tousled from sleeping, and handed Jean-François the phone.

He took the phone into the bedroom. The conversation with the person on the other end of the phone sounded like two old friends rediscovering each other.

The talking faded as Katie began thinking about all that had happened. She turned, dropping her gown, and stepped into the still-running shower. She loved the water spilling over her face while she was thinking.

Later, Jean-François walked back into the bathroom and told Katie they were leaving for Costa Rica.

***

Detective Darcy was sure the black Mercedes gang would be shadowing him as soon as he turned up a lead. It was no secret to Darcy or anyone with his years of experience that he was now Ramey's de facto front man, taking the lead to fight all the skirmishes, dealing with the red tape, and being a face to the press. Ramey could sit back and wait behind the scenes to swoop in for the prize Darcy unearthed.

Darcy spent the four-hour flight from San Francisco to Chicago and the half-hour elevated train ride from O'Hare to the Loop wrestling with his thoughts and questions. Darcy was about to head to the Palmer House Hotel, where the professor had booked a reservation, when he thought, *The grumbling stomach of a detective can't be ignored.* He stopped to grab some food at Pot Belly's Sandwiches.

His cell rang so loudly it startled him and the others waiting in line. "Detective? They're not in Chicago! They changed their tickets at the airport. And there's more. We just got confirmation they were on a flight to Costa Rica yesterday."

"And why didn't we know this before I took this sightseeing excursion?" Darcy railed.

As if not hearing him, the assistant grumbled. "That's right. They flew to Costa Rica, Detective. I checked the flight manifest, and they actually flew to San Jose, Costa Rica."

Back on the El to O'Hare, sandwich in hand, he stared out the window of the train. He watched the passing empty buildings of the Chicago suburbs while using his cell to call and make arrangements for a seat on the next flight to Costa Rica.

There were no flights out to San Jose until the following afternoon, so he took a room at the Airport Hilton. Before heading to his room, and suspecting Ramey was tracing his cell calls, he headed to a cell phone vendor in the hotel lobby to buy a pay-as-you-go untraceable phone. *They will have to work hard to keep up with me,* he thought.

A good sleep is always helpful, but he didn't get a good sleep that night. The next morning, long ticket counter lines and security at O'Hare didn't make for smooth sailing either. When he finally boarded the last plane that day and the plane was taxiing to runway 32-Right, he realized he had failed to get approval from his boss to chase this couple into foreign territory. He sighed. At some point he would call his boss, but he wanted to know more about this case first.

The small window in the 757, flying at 38,000 feet, was cold to the touch. He didn't like flying. "It doesn't feel right not having something underneath the plane to hold it up," he said, thinking out loud. Luckily, there was no one sitting next to him.

He fumbled with his ticket wondering, *Why this commotion about the digital pictures? What could these pictures be?*

Wait. I am pursuing photos. Why would the picture of some antiquity cause international concern? Why did this Berkeley professor think someone was about to be killed? Maybe the pictures were some scandal—like the museum director caught on film? Still doesn't make sense. His mind was running on two Vente Café Americanos when he noticed he had another layover in Houston. "Damn!"

He needed something to calm down. He would not eat on airlines, but he wanted a drink. They just weren't serving yet. *I don't care.* He rang the call button. As the plane trailed through the sky toward the equator, he became more and more disturbed. *Were foreign interests playing him for the sucker?*

He desperately wanted a cigarillo so he could really think this through. His fingers twitched and his right leg bounced to some internal jitterbug music. He tried to listen to the in-flight music, but his arm kept bumping the armrest button and changing the channel, frustrating him even more.

***

"What a life!" Jean-François said to Katie, looking at Clive's compound.

"I guess it pays to become an art dealer instead of an artist," Katie said.

"Maybe I should be a movie star instead of a professor?" Jean-François joked, pulling the cord to ring the bell.

Clive Merriweather had just finished building his home on 200 acres overlooking the Pacific on one side of the peninsula, with the bay on the other. The five structures that formed the compound included the massive 20,000-square-foot home that was occupied only by the staff most of the year. All the construction was old Spanish style, with red tile roofs and mud-style masonry walls. The massive wooden front gate that led into the compound was reminiscent of an English castle.

A tall, olive-skinned man turned the huge handle in the door of the larger ornate gate. Before Katie could say anything, she saw a short round man waddling in their direction. In their lamentable state, they were thankful for the cordiality and joviality with which this man threw himself at them. His pleasure in seeing Jean-François quickly became very lively.

Two years ago Jean-François had stayed at Clive's place, a large flat on San Francisco's Broadway Street in Nob Hill. He and Clive enjoyed talking about Middle Eastern art and the many subsequent artifact hunts to Egypt, which Clive funded.

"Hey, my friend, how was the trip? It's a fact that planes are uncomfortable flying cattle cars," Clive chuckled. "They never have enough Scotch to keep me sedated." Clive clasped his hands on Jean-François's shoulders and gave him the familiar European greeting. He turned, scanning Katie's body before giving her the same welcome.

Jean-François was somewhat puzzled by Clive's comment. He knew that Clive was a pilot and loved to fly. In Egypt, this short firecracker of a man would fly the three of them from site to site, searching for art in small desert villages. Shankara was the one who hated flying. As for Clive, flying through rough weather and landing on desert sand for an adventure was nothing to him.

"Clive, what are you talking about? Don't you love flying?" Jean-François asked.

"Sure, when I am in control!" he responded with a hearty laugh, followed by a cough.

Clive reminded Jean-François of the actor Sydney Greenstreet in *The Maltese Falcon,* a short, heavy, imposing man, with what could only be called shifty eyes. Clive liked to refer to them as bedroom eyes.

"Hey, Roscoe, take the bags. They must be tired from the trip," Clive said. "Guest suite, please, and we will see you both for dinner at five."

Jean-François hesitated. "Roscoe? That seems like a strange name for these parts."

"No, it's a TV name. Roscoe never liked his real name, Hector, so he picked one from the *Dukes of Hazzard* TV show. As a kid, he saw it playing in the window of a store in San Jose and heard the name. It stuck." Clive shrugged.

Roscoe showed them to a suite of rooms reminiscent of a Four Seasons hotel. The art was everywhere and clearly expensive, like the feel of Clive's estate. The large Venetian painting filling the wall behind the bed was surely sixteenth-century with bright red, green, and gold—vibrant colors. In the painting were a stylized man and woman in court attire; the man was juggling three silver balls. Katie and Jean-François both laughed and thought it was symbolic of their losing their marbles over this whole drama. They thanked Roscoe as he put their luggage in the large walk-in closet.

Dinner was, of course, impressive. The whole scene was right out of the pages of *Architectural Digest*. The large sumptuous dining room table was dwarfed only by the spectacular de Kooning's *Woman III* painting behind the table. It had fetched more than $100 million at an auction. Now Jean-François knew who the buyer was!

The conversation at dinner was polite and filled with stories of the two men's adventures in Egypt.

"How did you happen to call after so long?" Jean-François asked.

"Shankara was the one," Clive said. "She called me and said you needed a place to hang out for awhile."

"When did she call you? She didn't say anything to me."

"She called yesterday. Said you had just left."

Jean-François was pleased Shankara had made the call. He didn't ask anything more, as the travel, fine wine, and dessert made for fuzzy thinking.

***

The next day Jean-François was eager to start deciphering the language in the photographs, using a key Shankara had given him the day they left. He wanted privacy and a dark space so he chose the inside of the large walk-in closet at the back of their room.

He grabbed his "man purse," as Katie called it, from his duffel bag and unzipped the lower pocket, pulling open the lining and exposing the clear plastic bag of photos.

He stared through the bag at the photo of the pouch with the painted language on its fabric-like covering. Looking through the magnifying glass he'd brought with him, he compared the digital pictures to Shankara's language-deciphering key. He wasn't totally sure of what he was seeing, but his experience with this type of language was enough to help him, with the key, to begin to understand.

He studied all the photographs for more than three hours. Putting his thoughts together revealed somewhat of a story from the pictures. He drew a breath. *If this is true, I will indeed be famous, but I also will have every mercenary in the world after me as soon as word gets out.*

Jean-François called Katie from the pool area, where she was absorbing the sun. "You need to know this, Katie." He proceeded to the pool and sat next to her on the long chaise and began telling her his theory.

Katie sat stunned as he unfolded the amazing tale. "In the pottery jar there was a pouch containing three seeds from the apple tree in the Garden of Eden. Yes, *the* apple tree. Whoever saved this some thousands of years ago wanted it passed to a later generation and must have sealed it in the pottery jar that sort of fell into my hands. This jar and pouch must have been a very recent discovery." He thought about Dr. Mustafa. *Was there some relationship here?*

He showed her the bag with the photograph of the pouch on top. She stood up quickly and began pacing. She kept saying, "My God, are you sure?" Finally she came out of the shock. "That is more valuable than anything you can imagine. Christians, the Vatican, hell, the Israelis and Muslims are going to want this prize."

Jean-François broke in. "Here is another part I interpreted from the writing in the pictures I have been studying. This pouch was originally hidden by a camel driver crossing the desert."

After half an hour of talking, he pointed at an area on the pictures and said, "Here is the story. This is the point at which this mysterious old woman apparently drops a pouch while the camel driver is lying unconscious. That's what Shankara and I deciphered before we left for Chicago, well, St. Louis."

He paused. "Katie, this woman gave him a secret for someone in a future generation! It's a formula for a priestess or teacher to develop the ability to intuit and create in the world and then pass it on to others! See this part?" he motioned, pointing at a symbol in the picture. "It's a daily practice of this technique."

***

The professor worked on deciphering the formulas for another two days. By the morning of the third day, he had them figured out.

"Katie? I have the formulas! Sit there." He pointed to the chair next to the large patio doors. "The language in the jar, as we see in the pictures, sets up these processes about what seems to be what we would call intuition. It talks a lot about these cosmic rhythms." He paused, focusing internally.

Katie looked at him as if he were crazy and asked, "Are you OK? This sounds very superstitious."

He ignored the question and continued. "In normal conditions we receive the vibrations and rhythms of the great ocean of life through our intuition, and we respond to them. But in today's world we are so choked with information, hundreds of decisions daily, too much to do, old memories, and such that we fail to receive the impulse from what is called Mother Ocean. Consequently, disharmony and chaos manifest within us and all around us.

"This first process it describes helps us get in touch with that rhythm again so we can use it creatively. Each pulse beat, or heartbeat, is your rhythm and connects you to the rhythm of Mother Ocean. There is a part on the etching that says, 'One pulse or heartbeat is one unit.'" He paused.

"Great metaphor, isn't it?" he said.

"Here is the process—I'm calling it the Ocean Process. It's similar to a meditation with specific steps. Ready? Begin by closing your eyes. Now, close your right nostril with the right thumb and inhale through the left nostril for a count of six units." He could hear her labored breathing.

Jean-François continued reading the steps he had deciphered, guiding Katie through the process. Her breathing and countenance shifted with the inhalations and exhalations. After another fifteen to twenty minutes, Katie opened her eyes and said, "At first this was restful, then I got caught up in my mind chatter."

"Hmm. They must have anticipated this and developed this second process," Jean-François said. "It has you focus on spaces between thoughts until you can consistently be aware of what the writing calls "the gap." Close your eyes again, Katie, and try this—just like we were doing before. Without making an effort, try to bring your awareness to the silence or gap between your thoughts and hold it there or return to it."

Several minutes passed before Katie came back to the present and said, "I really feel like I moved into a silent, almost altered space. I don't know. My mind chatter and judgment seemed to disappear … I like it."

Jean-François nodded absentmindedly. "This next one I have labeled the Creation Process. The writing says that as you practice these steps, you will be able to set an intention based on an intuitive insight and create it using imagination and feeling. You sit in this silence for a time then ask your intuition what is needed and listen. Try it."

He took her back through the steps and added the ones for creating what she wanted. "The next step is to imagine it," he said. "Really see a picture or movie in your mind's eye. Once the image is firmly fixed, move it down into your heart to infuse it with feeling. Allow the image to come to life through this energy from the heart. I think it means this feeling and image vibration attracts similar energy in the material world."

Several minutes of silence passed. "The last part," Jean-François went on, "is to use your awareness to move the image from your heart region to the base of your spine. This is where the image generates the vibration of your imagination's vision and attracts the equivalent in matter."

Katie slowly came out of her trance-like state and said, "I think I get it, honey! When I went through the process, there was a point where it all felt very real. I also get why these thousand-year-old secrets could fall into the wrong hands and be dangerous!" She paused. "So this formula means anyone can create anything, right?"

There was no answer. Jean-François was already thinking about the fourth process. "This one—Remote Viewing Process, let's say—is to see a place or thing that is far away from you in space and time. You allow a vision to come into your imagination, paying full attention to all the detail in the vision: colors, people, environment, and things. You don't rush it. Hold the vision as long as you can while doing rhythmic breathing … ."

***

The older woman spoke softly to Clive, who was bent over Katie with Jean-François. "Dehydrated, she's dehydrated." The entire staff was crowded around. One of them ran out, returning with a small wet cloth. The woman slowly squeezed water out of it into Katie's mouth. Someone else came in through the veranda doors with a small green bottle of Gatorade. As the old woman poured a few drops of the Gatorade into Katie's mouth, she stirred.

She was awake again. The color was slowly returning to her face. "Doing better now?" Jean-François asked.

"When I passed out … " Katie replied, her breathing choppy. "I thought I could, like, hear a woman talking about our pictures."

Jean-François panicked and chased everyone from the room.

"You have to be careful, Katie!"

She was still in a haze. "She said that … it was the key to knowing … and she said … we are in danger from the … not from the Church."

"Katie? You were out. You couldn't have heard anyone say that; I have been here the whole time."

But she was very clear on this point, even though she still felt the fuzziness of passing out. He helped her to the edge of the bed and handed her the bottle of Gatorade from the nightstand. "Here, drink some more." Katie was sitting up but moving slowly.

They decided to take a slow walk along the beach. The path down from the crest of a hill overlooking the lagoon to a small beach was somewhat treacherous, and they had to stop from time to time. When they finally made it, they found a spot on the sand near the water and just sat.

"You know, I disagree with your earlier idea that it was someone other than the Church, Katie. Holy men 5,000 years ago were just like the ones today. To communicate with God, you had to go through them. These high priests have been guarding the gate of that knowledge. Power is what it's about. We all have intuition; we all just don't know it. To authentically create is a power we all have but are ignorant of! That's what the writing says."

His mood shifted. "Katie! Someone found this before we did but left the pouch inside the jar. The only other people who would have access to the vault were Dr. Mustafa and Ubaid."

Katie was overwhelmed with fear. She understood cultures, relationships, and societies, but having feelings was hard for her. She was much more comfortable in her left-brain world. Her mind began flashing through all that had happened in just a few days. Exhausted, she whispered, "I was right about this being a Da Vinci Code kind of thing."

She raised her voice. "Jean-François? Let's give the relic up. There is enough adventure already to write a book about. I'm really scared."

"At this point I don't think giving up the relic or giving the pictures back will stop them," he said, deciding not to tell her he no longer had the pouch. "I do think you're onto something about a book. Once the public knows this, Ramey and his gang, whoever they are working for, are less likely to target us."

"We have to get these people off our backs," Katie said, "and this might be the best place to do it. Let's just hide here. How long can we stay?"

"As long as we want," Jean-François replied.

***

Small things unsettled them. The water of the Pacific often was glaring as the sun slid toward the horizon, creating a harsh light that blanched everything they looked at. The wind periodically streaked through the trees and the outer door of their room, causing an irritating whistle and rubbing sound. When it happened, they would take a walk and practice the processes.

On one walk, the smell of a particular flower penetrated Katie's nose, mimicking the smell of her gardenia bush, making her homesick. It was also a reminder that her St. Louis flower garden didn't have a caretaker and their home had been left amiss.

"When can we leave and go home?" she asked in a homesick tone. Jean-François replied, "Let's walk and do the remote viewing." They picked an area outside the compound fence near the crest of the hill, deciding not to go to the beach.

"I can give you the instructions again if you need them."

"No, no. I can remember," she said.

They sat quietly, the sound of the water rhythmically rushing through the sand droning in the background. The air was crisp and clean, and the sun was beating onto their hats, causing more heat and sweat. Everything seemed to have a rhythm, so they started the rhythmic breathing.

Some forty-five minutes had passed when the experiment was abruptly interrupted. Jean-François jumped up in a panic. He shook Katie. He began telling her he had just seen a picture in his mind. "I saw a plainclothes police-man coming up the drive at the ranch house here. It was as real as life itself, Katie. Let's hide our stuff and head for the boat." He pointed down the slope at the dock below.

Clive's 60-foot boat was glaring in the sun next to the dark brown hue of the slip. The boat was well stocked with food and water. Clive always thought he would motor up the coast to California someday, but there was always a reason why he couldn't.

To the detective, this sun-parched land around the bustling city of San Jose was worse than the Nevada desert. Most of the trees had lost their leaves to the dry wind, and the roads were mostly dirt, washed out from heavy rains.

Darcy hired a cab to take him to the house. When he heard it was 130 kilometers from San Jose, his mumbled reply was, "Oh, God." He reached into his pants pocket for his cigarillos and pulled his new Costa Rican pack out. He drew back the foil and struggled to get a smoke from the flip-top box. The outside wrapper was much darker than American cigarillos and the tobacco heavier than his stateside brand. In fact, it irritated his lungs so much, he took one long drag and put it out.

Adding to the grouchiness of the trip were several large trucks driving on the rutted dirt road a couple of miles ahead. They stirred up clouds of dust, covering the roadside foliage with a dull brown layer in their wake.

Then the dusty hills unexpectedly became lush green jungle, reminding Darcy of pictures in the *National Geographic* magazines he used to thumb through during stakeouts or down time as a beat cop.

After the grinding four-hour drive, Darcy was hot and tired, but that didn't stop him from being amazed at the size of Clive's compound. Now he understood what the vendor near the art shop in San Jose was saying about getting the building materials and people over here to work: *must have been difficult.*

Darcy switched back to reflecting on how three days of snooping had led him to the professor and Clive's compound. *All my years as a cop, and yet, I never would have connected the professor and the art dealer had it not been for a talkative street vendor in front of that art shop.* The man had remembered the two North Americans who had asked about the art shop owner's whereabouts not long ago. The vendor said the owner was a North American too, an artist who had become world-renowned as an art collector while living in San Francisco.

Darcy had asked the vendor how he knew this information. The vendor was happy to tell him that just before this art dealer moved to Paquera, on the peninsula, he had bought the art shop and a rather large boat for making the trip across the bay from Puntarenas instead of having to take the overland driving route. Word eventually spread of this large house and compound as he began to build it. Vendors were renting barges to move the supplies from the mainland to Puntarenas then across to the peninsula.

Darcy stopped his daydream when the driver said that Clive's house was guarded. "Rebels from Nicaragua want to rob this place. They want money for their cause," he said. The cab pulled up in front of the compound's massive solid wooden gate. By the time Roscoe answered the gate, Jean-François and Katie had hidden their things in the jungle behind the house and made their way down the slope to the beach. Within a few minutes, they were in the boat and sliding up the inner bay.

Roscoe made Darcy wait while he brought Clive to the gate. Although the introduction seemed cordial, Clive wasn't about to tell this cop anything.

"So, you do not know these people?" Darcy said to Clive, who stood in the entrance of the gate.

"Sure, but I won't tell you where or when until you tell me what this is about," Clive said smugly. Darcy began telling Clive the story—or a version of it.

If Darcy had looked down from the hill where he was stalemated with Clive, the glassy bay water would have made spotting a boat easy. Plus, their boat was the only one on the bay. Jean-François stayed close to the shore, where the lush green trees and underbrush rushing down to the water's edge provided some distraction, especially in the breeze. He was moving slowly along the rugged edge, frequently looking up at the hill to catch a glimpse of anyone observing the boat.

He steered the boat over to the shoreline. "Give them about an hour. If it was a policeman who showed up, he should be gone. I'm sure Clive will confuse him and send him on his way," Jean-François said.

"What if he doesn't leave? What if it's not who you think it is?" Katie's voice was tense, and the pitch changed with each word.

"We have to find a way to sneak back and see if he's gone."

"I have your cell phone with me. Will it work?" Katie asked.

"Let's try." Jean-François took the phone and searched the contact list on it to find Clive's cell number. "Here, here it is." He dialed the number and listened. He remembered Clive saying cell communications were sporadic because it was so far out. The phone was silent. "I guess it's not working. I don't think it connected." He was not sure what to do next. Just as he was about to cancel the call, he heard a faint ring in the earpiece.

"Yes," burst the voice through the phone.

"Clive?" Jean-François said, not recognizing Clive's voice.

"Jean-François, what's this all about? What kind of trouble are you in?" Jean-François could hear Clive's anger.

Jean-François was worried the policeman might still be there and said, "Don't answer. Say 'no bananas today' if the police are still there. Then hang up and call this number back once he leaves."

"Jean-François! Jean-François! Stop being stupid. I sent the cop back to San Jose. What kind of stupid spy stuff is this banana crap? Jesus! What have you gotten into? Come on back. We need to talk. Now!"

ABDUCTION

As they walked up from the boat dock, Jean-François thought about how silly he had been in the last fifteen years. He was always on the lookout for some big event to validate him, gain approval, and show the world his genius. Now that this great prize was in his lap, he felt differently about it.

As they were approaching the compound, he half-expected someone to grab them and hustle them into a waiting car. Instead, Clive met them just on the other side of the large blue Spanish-tiled swimming pool.

Clive was steaming. He didn't like the police knowing about this place, he said. He chose his words carefully. This art dealer, world-renowned for his negotiating abilities, was subtly taking a position, appearing neutral while probing for more detail.

"Jean-François, how did you come across the relic?" Clive asked.

"So, the detective told you?" he asked.

"Yes, and he told me that he suspected this had less to do with this government and more to do with parties that act like governments."

"What does that mean? Did he tell you what I found?" Jean-François was fishing, hoping to glean what Clive and the detective knew.

"Not exactly," he said, turning away and walking toward the cabana.

Katie wanted to stop Jean-François from disclosing anything else. "Honey? Let's put on our suits and take a swim." Her tone was one of concern as she motioned for him to go inside.

"You go, Katie. I'll be just another second."

She spun around in upset, walking away in a huff, caught between her desire to change the direction of the conversation and her fear something might happen. On her way to the bedroom she crossed in front of the large glass veranda doors and noticed the reflection off the surface of the pool of a poorly dressed man with a pistol. He was in the bushes near the cabana wall. She continued without stopping, hoping not to be noticed. When she was far enough inside the bedroom, Katie ran to the other door and through the long hallway to the front of the house, panicked, to find Roscoe or a guard.

As she rounded the corner of the house, she and a guard collided. Out of breath, she tried to tell him, "Man? Gun … pistol … the pool!" There was the sound of a pop, and the guard pushed past Katie as they raced to get through the house to the pool.

The guard could see a man on the grass carpet at the edge of the pool. He ran, waving his gun, then slipped at the pool's edge. Catching himself, he saw his boss lying flat on his back, not moving. "Señor Clive?"

Katie made her way to Clive's side, opposite the guard. Blood was trickling down Clive's head into his jet-black hair and onto the ground, but she could see he was breathing. Terror, then numbness, spread through her whole body. "Jean-François! Where's Jean-François?" she yelled, as she cradled Clive's head in her arms.

There was no answer. Clive awoke a moment later. In the commotion he had fallen and cracked his head. He motioned for Katie to bend nearer. "Rebels," he muttered. "They have Jean-François."

***

The jungle was deep green and the heat and humidity so oppressive that Jean-François could barely stay on his feet. His lungs burned with each inhalation of moist hot air, and he had this sharp pain radiating from his right kidney area where the kidnapper had repeatedly jammed his gun.

Other than grunting and shoving the gun at Jean-François, the rebel had said nothing during the hours they plodded through the jungle. He kept waiting for a chance to break away or hit the man, but he was too sure-footed and never in an awkward position. The rebel was about three inches taller than Jean-François, but very thin, and, he guessed, the man was older.

He wondered what this torn-jeans-clad rebel wanted. *Did the detective hire one of the rebels to snatch him from the house? After all, this rebel seemed to know his way around. Maybe, he was a mercenary? No. He didn't look it.*

Then it came to Jean-François—*I am a ransom target. This rebel thinks I am Clive. He's going to take me back to where his gang will hold me for ransom. They think they have a famous art collector.*

Just as he completed this thought, he noticed the rebel stumble, begin to slowly twist, then fall. His face was contorted in pain. *Something is obviously wrong with him. But what? He no longer cares about me, so it must be pretty bad.*

He approached the guy cautiously and slowly reached for his gun. He noticed the rebel's eyes were distant, unfocused. He realized the chakra scan from the writings could help him determine this guy's problem. He scanned the rebel's body with his awareness, stopping at the area of the heart. Dark energy seemed to be slowly overtaking the entire heart area. *Heart attack,* he thought. He had gotten just enough of a look at the photos of the jar writings about medical intuition to know that he had to imagine white light flooding the heart region. He started by focusing on the gap between thoughts, then brought in the light. It wasn't easy with all his judgment and worry. He wasn't exactly sure if what he was doing was right, but he continued.

The rebel slowly began to respond. Jean-François couldn't tell at first, so he continued seeing white light flood the heart of this rebel. Looking down at him, Jean-François felt compassion for this man. He wasn't sure why— it didn't make sense—but he did. For the first time in many years, he was beginning to feel.

The dark area began to lighten and the rebel came back into consciousness and began speaking. Jean-François couldn't understand him and the man passed out again, but he had a feeling the guy would be all right.

Worried the rebel might want to take him in anyway, Jean-François left the area in a hurry. After an hour or so of running, he started thinking, *How exactly am I going to find my way back to the house? I have no idea how to return to Clive's compound. I don't even know if this rebel's gang is somewhere close.*

He had hoped to retrace their path, but the jungle had quickly covered the trail. *This was not a good sign.* A caution from the formula popped in his head: be careful of negative thoughts, as they multiply when focused on.

***

Katie sat at the pool bar nursing a white wine spritzer. Clive had a double Scotch in hand, but the ice was in a plastic bag against his head.

"What are they after? Do they know?" Katie asked.

"Katie, the rebels think they have kidnapped me and will most likely send a note asking for ransom money," Clive blurted out.

"What? No. You have no idea what Jean-François has found! It might be ... " Katie was feeling physically ill and moved over to the chaise to lie down. Clive motioned to a guard to come over. He whispered something and the guard left.

"The housekeeper and her assistant will take you to your room, Katie. Don't worry. I will have the native trackers find Jean-François."

Katie questioned in her mind what was going on but was still too stunned to care. It was all she could do to keep herself from passing out before she reached the bedroom.

***

Jean-François was tracing the path back through the jungle as far as he could, which wasn't far. The jungle light was changing all the time. The light was fading, and that meant night was near, with a whole new kind of jungle emerging. He heard the sounds shifting. Strong screeching noises were even stronger and more frightening than before.

My mind can make up stuff so fast.

He didn't know how much time he wasted, but twilight was beginning to cover the jungle. *I need to find a place to stop before all the light fades.* Finally, he just picked a relatively open spot and moved a lot of branches in a circle around the clearing. He layered twigs around the branches, figuring that would give him warning if something big approached in the dark.

By the time he finished, the light was nearly gone and he could feel his body tense with fright. He had never experienced this kind of world. Within an hour, it would be very cold.

What can I do?

First, he got angry. He was so close to breaking through and now he was breaking down. *Where was this amazing power now that I need it? I am not a field archaeologist with survival training.* His mind continued spinning.

How will I sleep?

How will I keep myself safe?

Can the rebels find me at night?

Can I build a fire? How?

Then he noticed a peculiar thought. *My mind is acting as if it's more frightened than I am.*

Wait! What?

I am confused. My mind is separate from who I am? It's not who I am? Right now I seem to be this witness of what is happening, witness to this mind and body. Curiously, they are in fear, but not the witness "me." I am not. I! What "I"?

I must be schizophrenic!

Jesus, what is happening?

He moved to sit near a large tree when a blinding flash of white light completely engulfed him. His mind went silent. He felt an amazing peace come over him, and there was a feeling of being one with everything. Then the jungle disappeared. There was no oneness; there was nothing. There was only peace. Everything disappeared into the white light, and just as quickly, it all returned to normal.

My mind is settled, and I am feeling this peace and complete confidence. There is no longer any fear.

Darkness more suited to a cave settled throughout the jungle. He thought about the episode where he had seen the detective coming to the house and wondered if he could use the same technique somehow now.

Then he heard a voice thundering in his head. "There is a power within you that you can use!" Obediently, he started with the breath work, allowing his intuition to work.

Then a word popped in. "Watch." He put all his attention on his mind's eye waiting for an image. *I know I can trust whatever follows next. A movie is starting. I am looking out of my eyes and seeing a path through the jungle. I ask my intuition a question: Am I moving through the jungle to Clive's house? The answer feels light and freeing. I watch the movie over and over again, paying attention to all the details.*

Several hours must have passed when he heard the thundering voice again. "Move!" As he did, he could feel the direction he needed to go. When he headed in the right direction, he felt light and he could see a path in his mind's eye. When he was off track, the vision simply grew darker.

By morning he had gone miles through the jungle, as if there was no such thing as time. Now he was halfway down the hill on the road leading to Clive's compound. He was thinking about the night he had just spent using the amazing technique. *Could my escape be the result of this formula? It is so hard to believe, and yet difficult to refute the evidence as I look at the compound.*

The sun's morning light began to filter through the last of the trees at the back of Clive's house. Jean-François heard a strange popping sound and felt something zing by his right ear. His heart jumped. *The guards are shooting at me!* He yelled out, "Clive, it's Jean-François!"

Within seconds several men appeared on both sides of him, with such threatening looks he was sure they were about to shoot. Clive shouted to them and motioned for them to bring Jean-François to him. Katie came running too, jumping into his arms and knocking him over.

"Jean-François, what happened? Are you all right?" Katie begged.

He whispered, "Are you?"

PANDORA'S BOX

"I know it's hard for you to believe this, Clive," Jean-François said, trying to explain what he had discovered. "It's about an ancient artifact, an inscription about intuition, and … "

Clive spat toward him, just missing his foot but hitting the pool. "It's the artifact that's priceless. I can't get a dime for that formula," he said. "That means nothing."

"Several hours ago I was mistaken for you and kidnapped!" I could feel my anger rising. "I found my way back here using a method that was carved inside the 5,000-year-old pottery jar, and you … think that is nothing?"

Clive yelled back. "I know exactly what this is about! How much do you want? Just tell me." Clive's whole body quivered, showing signs of stress.

Jean-François was dumbfounded at Clive's obsession with the object and his unwillingness to hear about his life-changing insight. As a professor, he had needed Clive's help in the early days, or so he had thought. It was really self-serving. *My need to be famous drove me. Now I feel repulsed by Clive, despite his supposed generosity.*

But that thought quickly gave way to feeling sorry for Clive. Jean-François could see his life was all about money and he might never know or accept anything greater.

"How much? For what? What are you talking about, Clive?"

"How long do you want to play this game? People are dying because … is that what you want, Professor?"

He thought, *Dying? I know about Ubaid, but that is one. What other people is he talking about? What is he saying?*

"Who has died, Clive? Who?"

He ignored Jean-François. "My cell phone is ringing. I need to go inside." Clive was anxious to answer his phone. Something was pulling his attention from the argument.

"We'll be there in a second," Jean-François said, motioning for Clive to go on in.

Katie rattled off a round of questions like a Gatlin gun. "Is there more to this? Is there a Pandora's box here? Once it's opened, will we regret it? The reason someone wanted this information protected is that it could be harmful, right? Who died? What is he talking about?"

Jean-François had no answers so he walked away, over by the living room windows, with Katie following. He noticed Clive pacing as he talked on his cell phone.

As they got closer to the door, Jean-François could hear part of the conversation. "I don't know! So where is it? And Shankara?" The wind was picking up, making a rustling sound through the open doors of the house and muffling the rest of the conversation. He had a sinking feeling.

He looked up at the billowing clouds, darkness against a darkening sky. Katie had left her shawl under the large tree near the pool, and she ran to get it before the rainstorm. "Be right there," she said, making it to the tree.

Katie grabbed the shawl and tried to pull it over her head, but it stuck, momentarily blinding her. She stumbled and ended sitting upright under the tree with the shawl around her head and shoulders. *This feels oddly familiar,* she thought. *Why?*

Jean-François joined Clive, who was still pacing around the house, his eyes bulging in anger.

"Clive, what's gotten into you? I've never seen you this angry," he said.

"You've been lying to me. What is the detective from San Francisco fishing around in a foreign country for? A digital picture or some formula? Come on! Dr. Mustafa, Ubaid, Shankara—all dead! Is that child's play?"

Pain ran through Jean-François's chest and took his breath away. He couldn't speak or move. Everything went dark as chills traveled up his back.

"Jean-François? I know what she meant to you. Wise up."

Jean-François was hurting, frozen in memories and pain.

Shankara! Dead! I can't believe it's true!

He was desperate and wanted to run, not caring about anything anymore. He was overcome and then several thoughts came in: *What have I done? What did I get her into? She's dead. And I can't say goodbye? Why?*

He stumbled over and sat on the gold-colored couch for several minutes, feeling only pain.

Moments later, Clive returned to their business. "Here are the photos," Jean-François said, motioning Clive over to the pool of light coming from a lamp by the windows.

"This is it? Why is Ramey so determined to get this? It looks like any other ancient jar," Clive said in disgust. "Jean-François, I don't care about the pictures!"

At the mention of Ramey's name, Jean-François suspected Clive was involved, if not the leader of whatever plot was unfolding. "Then is it the formulas you want?"

Clive was relentless. "Jean-François, you're an idiot! No one is chasing you for some formulas. It might be the most precious secret of intuition from heaven itself, but for your sake, come on. Where is the damn relic? Your lives are at stake!"

Jean-François was now sure Clive knew about the jar and pouch. He suspected Clive stumbled onto this information from discussions with Mustafa soon after Mustafa's discovery of the jar and relic. *Clive must have gotten close to Mustafa because of our expeditions to Egypt; he was always pumping him for information on his finds. He must have tried to make a deal.*

"I don't have it. I'm sure you know by now. It's in my lab in St. Louis."

"How would I know that?"

"You mentioned Ramey. Isn't that him and your thugs chasing me? Surely they have searched my place and lab there."

Clive sputtered, caught. "Do you realize this pouch is worth more than anything you could possibly imagine? Kings would send armies to capture this prize. My God!"

He moved to one of his library bookcases. Turning back to look at

Jean-François, he said, "I mean, we have known about intuition for a long time." He pointed to various books on the shelves. "And maybe we haven't understood how this 'creation' formula works, Jean-François, but you're saying there is something else beside the pouch that is … well, I don't buy it."

"How do you know what this pouch is about or what's in it, Clive?"

"I guessed based on what I heard through the grapevine and from Mustafa. I pieced that together with what you and Shankara have been saying and, oh, my God!" Clive snapped.

"If the detective who came to the house knows about this pouch, then every mercenary on the planet will be on the way here. There is a price on your head, Jean-François, in the millions. Millions! You have to leave. I'll protect you in my place in Abu-Dhabi."

Jean-François could feel Clive plotting. This was just another setup of some kind, trying to pressure him to turn over the pouch or keep him nearby until he could figure out how to get it.

The pouch, Clive, our trips through Egypt, Ramey, the man in black; it's all connected. Shankara. Oh, my God. She's really is, was involved. That's how they knew so fast where to find me in San Francisco.

Thoughts came at him quickly. *Oh, Shankara. I think in those early days I was searching for fame and attention. What were you searching for? What is it all worth when you are dead? Shankara, you and I were stupid.*

His anger at Shankara almost overwhelmed him. Then he heard Clive say, "Jean-François, I will get my plane ready, and in the morning we can go to your lab and retrieve the relic. Agreed?"

THE MYSTERY

As Jean-François was thinking through the whole scenario and his part in it, he came to the realization that maybe being Jerry Smith was OK. *And Jean-François … ah, I don't even feel like Jean-François anymore. Ironically, I'm now living in the world I wanted to be famous for, but it feels harsh and dirty.*

He looked toward the stone fence beyond the pool that formed its own horizon. *The air is muggy. That storm is heading in. Where is Katie?*

He could feel his eyes push through the expanse of dark, searching for her form. He flashed on his jungle experience and how he made it back to the compound using the remote viewing.

He called out, "Katie?"

There was nothing, so he called out again and heard a sound coming from the tree near the wall. He heard it again. This time he could make out her answering, "Here … I'm, I am here."

He ran to the sound, cutting the corner of the pool. The disk of the moon moved from behind a cloud and caught his eye. It was a perfect backdrop to the silhouette of a hooded person sitting motionless under the tree.

He wasn't sure who it was. *Another rebel?* "Katie?" he called again.

She responded in a deep, trance-like voice. "What is it?"

He could feel his heart pounding as he reached her.

"Katie? Katie? Are you all right?"

He felt a chill run up his spine as he saw the dark form.

"Oh," she said softly. "What happened?"

He took her by the arm into the house and announced to Clive that they were headed to bed.

"Good idea," Clive said. "We leave for St. Louis at 7 a.m."

He helped Katie walk down the hall toward the bedroom, passing the two sculptures from Michelangelo's apprentice period that were surely worth untold millions. He led her into the bedroom and closed the door.

"Clive is the mastermind of this whole thing," Jean-François said. "If the phrase 'follow the money' is true, here is our leader."

He headed for the bathroom. "You know, Katie, these old mystics were a lot smarter than anyone thought. Look at the trouble we are in."

A deep trembling came over him, followed by a rush of thoughts.

How long had Shankara been involved? Was she Clive's lover? He choked, his stomach vibrating. That would mean she was just after the money too. Oh, Shankara!

He was nauseated by his thinking and leaned over the sink while he looked in the mirror into his eyes. Then he said, "eye of the heart."

He wasn't sure where that came from. He was tired and his thoughts were jumping around. He didn't know what to do with these feelings about Shankara.

"Eye of ... seeing with the heart?" Katie said from the bed. "That's intuition, isn't it?"

He looked back over his shoulder at Katie, realizing he'd spoken out loud. "Yes, you're right. 'Eye of the heart' is intuition."

"Tell me more about the pouch."

Jean-François moved to the bed and took Katie's hand. "Well, the pouch and the writing on it and the jar are about creating. The Garden of Eden story is not about the 'creation' story but the 'creating' story.

"Katie, you were right in your previous suspicion. The reason for allowing only certain people to know these formulas on intuition, remote viewing, and creating must be the Pandora's box syndrome. If any thought could manifest, a person might hurt another.

"So the formulas are about using our intuition to guide us. Intuition plus imagination, plus feeling, manifests in the world."

Katie was quiet, thinking about his words. As he started to remove his shoes, he heard his inner voice say, "Call the detective."

"Katie, I need to make a call."

Katie nodded OK and headed for the bathroom. Jean-François had nabbed the detective's business card off the visitor's plate in Clive's foyer and instinctively put it in his shirt pocket behind the plastic protector.

Now he pulled it out and dialed the number. While the phone was ringing, he took the pocket protector out, staring at it for a moment and reflecting on how contrived it felt. He tossed it into the trash.

"Can I speak to Detective Darcy? Can you get a message to him? OK. What's the cell number?" He dialed the new number. It was taking a long time to connect, but a man finally answered.

"Detective Darcy? This is Jean-François … yes. Can you meet me at the airport in San Jose, Alitalia counter? OK."

Katie came back into the room as he finished. "Can you piece this whole story together for me?"

"To start with, I have learned a lot about myself, Katie," Jean-François said. "When I first discovered the writing in the jar, I knew this was the fame I always wanted. When I took the pouch, I knew I was doing something wrong. I was thinking only of myself.

"I didn't realize that there was this network of supposed friends that were conspiring. But it makes sense that I would attract others who have that same kind of selfishness and insecurity. They were just more …"

"How do you feel about it now?" Katie interrupted.

"All I have gone through has opened my eyes. I realize people need to know about this find. The need for fame, for me, disappeared back in the jungle. Then as I untangled this discovery, I wanted everyone to know they are powerful beyond their dreams."

"What about the pouch and seeds? I don't understand the whole story about the pouch and seeds," she said.

"From all the sources related to the jar, the writing on the inside of the jar, and on the pouch, and using Shankara's deciphering key, it appears that the seeds represent the seeds of creation."

"You mean the real seeds from the Garden of Eden?"

"At least from the Garden of Eden period. I remember reading about work done by several teams in the 1970s who thought the garden was in an area known as Dilmun, which is Bahrain today.

"The pouch pictographs are from the period of the garden story, and it says it's a place also called Dilmun. Then it says the first seed represents Intuition. The second seed represents Intellect. The third represents Instinct.

'When we got to St. Louis, before coming here, I sent the pouch and seeds to the DNA lab at Saint Louis University. The lab test showed that each seed has a different DNA structure—none of which has ever been seen before.

"The DNA of each seed shows the traditional structure of 10 percent for building proteins and 90 percent as programmable limitless possibilities. It also contains the original blueprint of this universe.

"By the way, I had them FedEx the seeds back to me at the lab of Tommasso Gambino at the Vatican, where we are heading next for some additional testing."

Katie had fallen asleep somewhere in his explanation. Jean-François smiled down at her then got up and began packing for both of them.

Dream Time

Katie had been dreaming a lot since they started this trip. This night, Katie flew across an expanse of desert, approaching an old rock monastery perched on the side of a hill near a village. She glided into a room filled with candles and was confronted by a strange-looking, hooded person sitting as if in meditation.

Katie landed right in front of the person.

"Let me tell you a story," this person said.

Even in the dream, Katie wondered at the significance of this faceless being. There was a loud thump, and Katie woke up. Sitting up in bed with a start, she said, "Jean-François?"

"What? What's wrong?" He moved quickly from the patio door to her side of the bed and sat holding her. "Are you OK?"

"I had this strange dream. There was a person with no face trying to communicate with me."

"What?"

"I flew across the desert and floated into this rock monastery. There was a being with no face. I don't know," she paused. "Somehow it felt familiar. This presence was very familiar. I asked if there was a reason for not having a face, and the answer was, 'You will know soon.' "

Jean-François had quietly moved their luggage down to Clive's boat a few minutes before. He and Katie now reached the boat and motored across the bay to Puntarenas where the ships came to port. From there, they found a bus heading to the San Jose International Airport.

***

They were walking to the Alitalia counter when Jean-François saw a man approaching who looked exactly like the detective in his meditation. He could feel his heart pounding. "Darcy?" he asked.

"Yes. It's Detective Darcy, Professor. So, what's this about? Usually when suspects call me, that means there is a story, an explanation they want me to hear. Or maybe evidence that they didn't do what everyone is saying they did. Which is it for you?"

"First, Katie had nothing to do with ... "

He was interrupted by the detective. "Never mind. Actually, I know the story. I know it all."

"How?"

"Shankara."

"What? I thought she was dead?"

"She called us after Ramey and the others were in her office in Berkeley. Best thing she could have done. Smart woman! She was in over her head. They threatened to kill you if she didn't go along with the plan."

Alive? Shankara is alive? Jean-François was shaky but happy she was alive. It took him a minute to take in the full impact of Darcy's words. Paradoxically, he then started to feel more distant toward her. All the emotional connection with Shankara was different now. *She betrayed me, set me up, then betrayed them—like a double spy. Who is she?*

He was surprised by a sudden flood of stories about human sacrifices that came to mind: Biblical stories, Aztec and Trojan myths, and others. About the same time, an amazing realization came to him. These stories were about symbolic sacrifices not real ones. It wasn't about a human sacrifice to release the soul from the body, but about sacrificing the ego to release the soul from the ego/mind's clutch.

If, as the Bible says, the sins of the father are visited on the son, then it means all the ego expectations of my father became my ego's duty. I took on my father's needs and fears, his wants and desires. I have been doing the same thing as Shankara. I have really been two people—Jerry and Jean-François. Jean-François was my ego's desire for recognition and approval

***

Darcy waited and watched Jean-François. When he could tell the professor was back in the present, he continued. "That last call you overheard at Clive Merriweather's was likely between him and Ramey, the man in black.

It was a setup using Ramey, who we had in custody by then. We needed Merriweather back in the USA so we could arrest him. That call set the wheels in motion. Of course, we have people stationed at his local airport, the St. Louis airport, and your lab. Doubt he can get away."

"What will happen?" Jean-François asked.

"With Shankara, you mean? With all this international stuff, laws, and such, the museum decided not to file charges against her. They wanted Merriweather and his thugs. She might originally have been greedy, but she wasn't a killer or even a big-time player," Darcy responded. "She just didn't know who she was. Too immature. "

***

On the final leg of the journey, when planes make people feel more like cargo than passengers, Katie stirred from a nap.

"Beauty sleep?"

"Jerry," she said, groggy, almost semiconscious. She started to correct herself when Jean-François interrupted. "Never mind. The name isn't important. I have learned the difference between being an actor and being authentic." His voice fluttered, and he looked away, unused to his own tears.

"My dream, remember? The hooded person? This time, she was sitting under a tree in the desert. And it was the same being. I could feel the same presence, Jerry, that I felt in my dream the other night. I know who it is!"

"Who? Who is it?" He was so eager to know.

"Me! I'm the hooded monk, the wise woman in the desert," came her reply. "And you are the camel driver! I gave you the secret and pouch to hide until we arrived at this time and place and could use it to help people."

EPILOGUE

Katie and I realized that we traveled from 5,000 years ago to this time period so we could bring this information to the world: a world more open and understanding about using these powers properly.

There are some things that are outside the grasp of intellect. But we can use intuition even if the mind doesn't understand how it works, where it comes from, or much else about it. In the coming years we will use our intuition more and more, and humanity will rediscover one of the original gifts of Spirit beyond our symbolic languages.

It is our duty now to bring this forth into the world without religious or political concerns. On a cosmological timescale, human beings are still barely out of the womb. Humans have progressed very little in their humanity and compassion for each other. Some have discovered the higher path, as Katie and I have done. There is much for us to discover about ourselves and our inner world. It is time go exploring our inner depths, and Katie and I are leading the exploration.

I believe that the next hundred years will astonish everyone. Spirituality will be about our inner world and religion about the outer structures. The language of that outer world is the symbolic language of the intellect. And the language of the inner world is Intuition.

Welcome to the new world!

The Science of Intuition

The Research

Knowledge has three degrees—opinion, science, illumination. The instrument of the first is sense; of the second, dialectic; of the third, intuition. —Plotinus

As I travel the country facilitating workshops about intuition and healing, I have found most people want to believe in intuition. Because our highly technological, scientific, rational society tends to dismiss intuition as unreliable, unscientific, intangible and spooky, they hesitate.

The rational left-brain is the gatekeeper of the unconscious. It requires an acceptable reason to believe in intuition or to become motivated to practice intuition. There are two ways of developing this acceptable reason: one is to have a powerful direct experience of intuition. This gives the left brain proof-positive. The second way is to provide enough rational understanding so the linear mind accepts, at least, the possibility.

Although science tends to disregard intuition, Michio Kaku's book *The Physics of the Impossible* is filled with examples of what science finds impossible today but possible in the future. Quantum physics of the early twentieth century was initially dismissed, yet it changed the paradigm of physics, even when physicists said there was nothing more to discover in that field.

As a person who has developed intuition and as a writer, I want to clear up some of the confusion that exists about the subject. To do this, I use personal experience, psychology, and physiology. By seeing the scientific research in the area of brain/mind, perhaps you will also feel more comfortable about the power you have, called intuition. But remember, the scientific understanding of brain/mind is rapidly changing.

Laura Day, best-selling author practicing and writing about intuition, was tested by a group of scientists in Rome when she was a young woman. The scientist and doctors in the room wanted her to demonstrate her intuitive abilities for the esteemed panel. All were highly impressed. In her book *Practical Intuition* she writes, "I have been tested on many other occasions, and since that time I've developed a career as a practicing intuitive."

The past devastating judgments by society linking intuition to something evil or insane are also changing. By taking a casual approach to the topic rather than a scientific dry one, I trust you will be able to conclude that you have the power of intuition, understand why sometimes it doesn't work for you, and feel as if developing your intuition is OK.

In this section, I have chosen to focus on the science of intuition. I show that intuition is vastly more common than most people believe and that it is a function higher than the mind. It is, therefore, impossible to completely understand, yet it is very practical in everyday life.

I ask my students and workshop participants, "What is intuition?" Some answer that it is a "gut-level feeling"; others say, "a hunch" or "Higher Self." Some believe "it's dead people talking" or "angel guides." We will answer this important question in this section.

> *If at first an idea does not sound absurd, then there is no hope for it.* —Albert Einstein

THE BRAIN

Although using intuition doesn't require any understanding of the mind, clearly our Western culture has become fascinated with the mind and thrives on intellect. The evidence is the myriad self-help and mind/brain science books, magazines, and DVDs sitting on bookstore shelves.

The brain is not the mind. According to Karl Pribram, M.D.:

> *I don't like the term the mind, because it reifies—that means it*

makes a thing of—something that's a process. We pay attention, we see, we hear. Those are all mental processes, mental activities. But there isn't a thing called the mind. There might be something you want to call yourself, but the mind sort of makes something concrete out of something that's very multifaceted.

Psychological studies during the early nineteenth century opened the doors to this newfound science called psychology. Cognitive (how we think) experiments in the late 1800s were taking place in the field by William James at Harvard and Sigmund Freud in Europe. But in the late 1920s, the study of the mind and cognition was considered to be nothing more than romantic illusions. According to the work of behavioral psychologists such as J.B. Watson and B.F. Skinner, human behavior as a function of environmental history and reinforcing consequences was more important than mental processes. These behavioral reinforcement processes were emphasized by Skinner and were seen as primary in the shaping of behavior.

This concentration on behavior didn't really change until the 1960s, when the direction shifted away from behavioral study and toward cognitive psychology again.

Further growth was evident in the 1970s and 1980s as other branches formed in psychological research. Neuropsychology, for example, began the study of how the mind creates internal representations of the external world. It explored thought, memory, perceptions, learning, and reasoning, with less emphasis on behavior.

Although behavior was much easier to study because of the obvious external modeling, when various imaging systems and computers came into the research labs, neuro studies soared.

The biggest contribution to these studies over the last thirty years has been the ability to examine the brain with new and powerful tools such as Functional Magnetic Resonance Imaging (fMRI) and Positron Emission Tomography (PET) Scanners. Both allowed researchers to watch a person's brain processes live, in real time. Within the last fifteen years, these systems have become so fast they can map brain activities scientists thought permanently inconceivable. The results were stunning and led to more exploration of the way the brain memorizes, reasons, and learns, with fascinating results.

Today these various types of imaging systems are yielding powerful maps of the brain and related electro-chemical-mechanical reactions. These advances are providing links that demystify the operation of the mind and its correlation to our strange gray-matter, Jell-O-like mass called the brain.

Brain Structure

Brain mapping has been around since the early 1800s, but today, with the remarkable new equipment, our brain maps are much more complex.

The brain is the physiological three-pound bio-mass inside the head, whereas the mind consists of subjective mental processes. Rather than give you a detailed breakdown of the biological gray matter, I want to summarize the main parts and correlate their functions, so later, when we discuss intuitive types, you will have some background for understanding them.

The *lower brain* is also known as the brain stem, reptilian brain, or action brain. This is the oldest evolutionary part of the brain—perhaps the first brain of the human species. The mental processes of this part of the brain are unconscious. Its function is related to instinct.

The lower brain is the biological operation center of the brain. It controls the breath, heart rate, and digestion, and includes the cerebellum, which coordinates senses and muscle movement, hence the title "action brain."

Another area found in higher primates is the *midbrain*. This is actually a group of brain structures that contain links between the lower brain and the hypothalamus; it also manages certain drives and actions through the hormone system.

The *limbic brain* is also known as the emotional brain and controls the hippocampus portion of the brain. It is through the hippocampus that memories are managed. Without the hippocampus, there would be no memory;

we could only live in the now. Without the rest of the limbic system, we simply would not be able to determine which emotions are important.

The *thinking brain*, or cortex, is about 80 percent of the brain's mass, although that doesn't mean we use 80 percent of it. It is still the most mysterious of this amazing Jell-O like thing and plays a key role in memory, attention, perceptual awareness, thought, language, and consciousness. The area known as the prefrontal lobe of the cortex is responsible for most of our high-level executive functions (as they are called by psychologists): judgment, planning, and morality. These functions relate to our abilities to determine good and bad, better and best; differentiate among conflicting thoughts; and project future consequences of current activities, to name a few. This is the area of the brain we call conscious.

Changing the Brain

Martha Curtis plays an amazing melody from a Beethoven symphony. Thirty minutes later she awakens from a grand mal seizure. Martha is a thirteen-year-old musically gifted violinist who began playing at age nine. Although she began suffering convulsions shortly after she was nine, she managed, with medications, to graduate from music school and play with various orchestras. After years of medication, she suffered four grand mal seizures, some while she was performing onstage.

More frightened and exhausted, she looked for epilepsy experts. By the time she saw the doctors at the Cleveland Clinic, her condition had become life-threatening. In the doctors' opinion, the only way to stop the traumatic seizures was to remove the portion of the brain causing the problem.

The doctors told her they were hopeful about the operations but skeptical that Martha would be able to play the violin again. Finding no other options, the doctors operated immediately, removing one-quarter of her right brain in the area where scans indicated electrical disturbances were taking place.

Anxious to prove to herself and others that it was possible for her to play Beethoven following surgery, she scheduled and performed a concert for family, doctors, and friends. In spite of everyone's fear she performed magically. The astonished doctors began wondering how this was possible and began further research into her condition.

The seizures continued in spite of the operations, and ultimately, Martha returned to the Cleveland Clinic where the puzzled doctors ran more tests. Again they found more electrical disturbances in the remaining areas of the right brain. Again they decided more of her right brain would have to be removed. After this operation more than a third of her right brain had been removed.

This time the recovery period was longer, and even though Martha was eager to play her violin, she was forced to wait. Finally she began practicing. And again, to everyone's awe, she played as if nothing had happened.

Doctors were bewildered. Considering that the right brain accounts for musical ability, the question of how Martha could continue to play with seemingly little or no effect intrigued the brightest medical minds. After considerable research and family history, the doctors concluded that a fierce case of childhood measles Martha had contracted at age three had actually damaged much of her right brain. As the doctors continued their study, they recognized that the damaged three-year-old brain had reorganized itself. It had shifted responsibility of some right-brain functions to another area of her left brain. The mystery of removing so much of her right hemisphere without damaging her musical ability was solved. Jeffrey M. Schwartz, M.D., and Sharon Begley recounted this story in their book *The Mind and the Brain*.

The story above shows the mistaken long-held belief that the brain's development is static throughout life. What we have thought was impossible might be a simple lack of information.

It was Freud's psychoanalytic theory of personality that brought the idea of the unconscious mind to the forefront when he suggested it is a reservoir of feelings, thoughts, urges, and memories outside of our conscious awareness. Although he suggested these were suppressed and negative in nature, current psychoanalytic theory does not support this view.

Defining the unconscious mind is touchy because there is very little agreement within the various scientific disciplines. That said, for our purposes, the unconscious mind can be defined as mental phenomena that a person is not aware of at the time of their occurrence. These phenomena include feelings, automatic skills, perceptions, thoughts, habits, beliefs, phobias, and desires unknown to the conscious mind.

In school I learned that certain areas of the brain are responsible for controlling specific parts of the body. The right brain controls the left side of the body, and the left brain controls the right body side.

The brain is a complex nerve center connected to a bio-physical mass called the body. It relays information to and from the body's organs, limbs, senses, etc. In some scientific circles it is analogous to a transceiver, both sending and receiving data.

I have always believed, as others have, that the functions attributed to the right brain and left brain were hardwired. For hundreds of years, this theory that the brain develops in childhood and becomes static as you become an adult has pervaded scientific theory.

Science is changing. Recent research has given us a new term: neuroplasticity, the self-organizing ability of the brain to form new neural connections throughout life. Neuroplasticity means the neurons in the brain compensate for injury, disease, and/or changes in beliefs.

A study conducted in 1990 by researchers Jenkins, Merzenich, Ochs, Allard, and Guic-Robles was published in the *Journal of Neurophysiology*. Their lab experiments demonstrated the programmability of the brain when damage occurred to the nerves of the thumb and fingers. This loss of electrical activity in the nerves caused a correlated segment of the brain's cortex to go dark and lose activity. This brain area shut down because it lacked the sensory input from the thumb/finger.

The groundbreaking part of the experiment came by accident. The researchers had to stop their work, so it wasn't until ten years later that they checked the experimental animals and discovered that the region of the cortex that originally had gone dark was then receiving input from nerves in the cheek! Here was evidence the brain actually reorganized itself.

Sharon Begley, in her book *Train Your Mind, Change Your Brain,* says:

A brain with no special ability in sports or music or dance might be induced to undergo a radical rezoning, devoting more of its cortical real estate to the circuitry that supports these skills.

Change requires clear attention, intention, and discipline, as seen in Dr. Schwartz's work with individuals with obsessive-compulsive disorder (OCD). In *The Mind and the Brain,* he reported success in changing OCD patients' patterns through a modified Buddhist process of awareness, or mindfulness. For ninety minutes a day, for as many as sixty days, patients focused their awareness or attention on the compulsive thought causing their problem and repeatedly said to themselves, "This thought is erroneous." Dr. Schwartz found the patients had a decrease in those thoughts. The mind/brain was adapting.

MIND

Three Levels of Mind

Let's explore the domain of the mind with a brief investigation into the philosophical levels of mind with the most influence on our lives: intellect, instinct, and intuition. The first two definitions are from *wordnet.princeton .edu;* the third one is from the online *Concise Oxford English Dictionary.*

Intellect

Intellect: reason: the capacity for rational thought or inference or discrimination [within our awareness].

Although the brain is one of the most complex structures in the universe, the mind, distinct from the brain, is still difficult to define. Even after millennia of philosophical pondering, new and powerful testing equipment, and current neuroscience, there is little agreement across science disciplines in classifying the makeup of mind.

There is some agreement among cognitive psychologists, and they catalog the mind's internal processes as feelings, reasoning, imagination, linguistics, and verbalization. Of these, let's concentrate on imagination, linguistics, and verbalization and call them our intellect.

Imagination is also known as the faculty of imagining and is our ability to form mental images without perceiving through senses, i.e. sight, hearing, or other senses. Imagination helps provide meaning to experience and understanding to knowledge; it is, therefore, a fundamental faculty through which people make sense of the world.

Linguistics refers to the mind's ability to interpret language in terms of the concepts that underlie its forms. This includes processes of understanding grammar, meaning, and combinations of words.

Verbalization refers to the mind's ability to take thought energy and convert it to language that can be spoken or communicated in some way.

To summarize, the intellect is comprised of imagination, linguistics, and verbalization. Furthermore, it analyzes and chooses, and is self-aware.

Instinct

Instinct: inborn patterns of behavior often responsive to specific stimuli.

Instinct is that part of you that is millions of years old, is your unconscious processes, and because it is silent, is difficult to pinpoint. Today scientists tend to agree the reptilian brain or R-Complex is the seat of instinct. Without it, we would not understand the basics of life, such as why it is important to flee from an oncoming car or tiger. Or how to even beat our heart.

The autonomic nervous system might be called instinct because it regulates the body's many activities and requires no conscious choice. The body could never rely on the fickle out-loud intellect to manage its various functions through its process of choosing. Imagine the more than 10,000 chemical reactions per second necessary for the body's survival. Now imagine the intellect managing these processes—it is hardly stable enough to operate a couple of these actions. That's why all vital functions of the body are managed by instinct: breath, pulse, and liver, bladder, and cell function, for instance.

Before we go further, I would like to clarify the term subconscious mind, which is a popular term but generally frowned upon by the psychological community because of the confusion that exists around the "sub" prefix of the word. This could refer to a topographical position or lower ranking (as in not as good as the conscious mind). Unconscious is the appropriate term and means "beyond awareness." In contrast to the intellect's verbalized thought, instinct is part of the unconscious mind and therefore outside of our awareness.

A well-known early contributor to this subject of the unconscious mind was Dr. Sigmund Freud, arguably somewhat off in some of his science, but a pioneer of freeing consciousness from physiology. He gave us the concept of unconscious mind and separated mind from brain. And in many ways, eighty to ninety years later, his work provided a jumping off place for other groundbreaking fields of study, such as Neuro-Linguistic Programming (NLP), cognitive neuroscience, and similar fields. Each in turn has given us various insights into the operation of the unconscious mind, of which instinct is a part.

Summarizing, instinct is our beyond-awareness automatic behaviors, fight or flight patterns, and control of the automatic bodily functions.

Intuition

Intuition: the apparent ability to acquire knowledge without inference or the use of reason.

Research into intuition by psychologists, psychotherapists, and neuroscientists began in earnest in the early 1960s. A few studies were covered in the media, but most of the work stayed in the academic community. It finally reached Main Street in the 1980s when the phenomenon called "medical intuition" became news. Since then, it has steadily gained popularity.

Because of this acceptance, more people are asking the question, "What is intuition?" I gave you dictionary definitions, and here is another compiled from several sources: An answer that is not logical, scientific, and rational; it is receiving the right answer without any accurate supportive data.

A similar definition is found in the book *Awakening Intuition* by Mona Lisa Schulz, M.D., Ph.D., as "… the process of reaching accurate conclusions based on inadequate information." Is it any wonder it is so confusing?

There are many questions about intuition that our intellect would like answered also: What is intuition? How does it work? Why doesn't it work all the time? Where does it come from? How is it different from instinct?

For most of our history, myth, folklore, and fiction have dominated this astonishing yet very human capacity. Phrases like "it's a woman's thing" or "something witches do" or "only a high priest can do it" or "only the gifted have it" have been used as another way of identifying intuition (sometimes with judgment or without) for decades.

Most often schooling has ruled out intuition as a legitimate process. We have been so indoctrinated into critical thinking (referring to thought processes that evaluate information such as accuracy, logic, fairness, and clarity of conclusions) and left-brain processes that they have become the dominant force in education and daily lives. I hope to clear up some of these outmoded concepts and help you realize that you and everyone else have the ability to be intuitive. If you understand intuition, to the limit the rational mind can, you will certainly begin using your greatest gift.

I call intuition a gift because it is so special in and of itself. Yet it is not a gift that is selectively given! Everyone has it and everyone used it in childhood, before the rational mind developed. And everyone can learn how to use it again.

Marcia, a former bank executive, participated in a workshop I facilitated on the subject of discovering our natural gifts. Intuition is the main influence and training of my workshops, each of which is focused on specific areas, such as business, health, etc. Marcia hoped to discover her "real life purpose and gifts." As she worked through the exercises, she recognized that she had thoughts and feelings "out of the blue" that were accurate but that she dismissed because they could not be explained or substantiated until much later.

Over the next months, Marcia recognized these patterns of dismissing what came up as illogical and changed the behavior by practicing her intuition until she was clear about how it worked for her. Today she is a successful business intuitive or as she prefers a "business consultant" who utilizes her intuition. She is helping companies and executives solve problems and learn to use their intuition as a powerful guide to their own success.

Here is the conundrum: the intellect can never understand intuition because intuition is beyond (or higher) than intellect. Although intellect wants and needs a logical, rational, and scientific explanation for intuition, intuition is not logical, rational, or scientific. Intuition comes from a higher level of mind than intellect, which is why the left-brain reasoning mind has difficulty understanding it. Having no apparent cause or quantifiable process, intuition can't exist, says the intellect.

However, the experience of hundreds of thousands of people says intuition does exist, and this is where the confusion between intellect and direct experience takes place. Our experience can be dismissed by the rational mind and those who doubt intuition. This is why having a personal experience, undeniable to you, is so important.

Perhaps like me, you remember a time when you got the right answer to a math problem but couldn't prove how you knew that it was right. The mind just can't do an adequate job of explaining or even accepting what is beyond its grasp. That's the reason intuition has been dismissed for countless centuries.

At best the intellect can sense a gap in thinking through which intuition flows. The gap is the silence or space between thoughts. Since we are used to having strings of thoughts leading to other strings of thought, it is hard for us to witness the gaps between the strings.

Just because it is difficult to quantify doesn't mean science is totally ignoring it. Science does, however, look at it as a nearly insurmountable problem because there is so much difficulty in predicting intuition, and there seems to be no formula or observable cause, and no way to quantify or measure it against some known conscious process, scale, or metric.

Nevertheless, new studies are under way and yielding fascinating results. Research at the Institute of HeartMath (see page 90) suggests that the seat of intuition is at or near the heart. The investigators found when intuitive insights were detected, electrical circuits near the heart fired prior to the circuits of the brain. This would indicate that the heart is directly involved in intuition, prior to the brain taking part. In our "Secret of Knowing" story the hooded woman in the desert says, "You can't always believe the eyes in your head; you can, the eye of your heart," meaning intuition.

In the early twentieth century, metaphysician, lecturer, and author Dr. Ernest S. Holmes wrote in his 1928 edition of the *Science of Mind* textbook, "The doorway to the Absolute stands open at the center of our intuitive perceptions." Later he says, "The Spirit of man seems to have an external and an internal perception. Its external perception is by appearance; its internal, through intuition."

Francis Vaughan, pioneering transpersonal psychologist and author, wrote in her book *Awakening Your Intuition:*

> ... [It] is known to everyone by experience, yet frequently remains repressed or undeveloped. ... Developing the intuitive faculties

allows one to recognize the possibilities inherent in any situation.

Although very few studies are specific about how intuition works, experiential data do tell us it is not limited to any culture, education level, or religious tradition.

Unconscious Mind

According to Steven Pinker in his book *How the Mind Works,* a set of experiments from researchers in the field of neurophysiology found that an electrical current flashed in the lower brain before a firing in a muscle in the arm took place. The cortex or conscious brain did not "order" the arm to move until after this brain stem signaled the arm. These puzzling results lead back to the question of what stimulated the event. Is the unconscious somehow placing the order to the conscious mind?

In another similar study in 1982, R.A. Coaster suggests that "conscious will" might be an illusion. Using high-speed fMRI images, PET scans, and computers on the mind/brain, it was discovered that conscious thought does not always start a decision-making process. Conscious will or volition—*I think I will have that second cup of coffee*—actually takes place nanoseconds after the muscles' electrical circuits have already started receiving an activation signal from another part of the brain to reach for the cup.

Which comes first then, the desire of the conscious mind or the unconscious one? We easily slip into the domain of philosophy and spirituality with questions like: Who or what is it that wants the second cup of coffee? Who am I if my conscious will is an illusion? If it is the unconscious mind starting the process before the conscious mind, does that mean there is another hidden controller?

The unconscious mind's nature is to process according to prearranged patterns, like applications software on your PC computer. Said another way, the unconscious mind is a creature of habit. When thought, experience, and emotion combine, they "groove" the brain, forming tracks for the thought to run on effortlessly in the future. The intensity and volume of similar thoughts cause the release of a set of chemicals, called neurotransmitters, which end by building a strong synaptic area (junction) that supports that groove. The secret of all real power is to form the habits and grooves of success. A strong fear around a subject, for example, might have such intensity that deep grooves are formed quickly and easily recalled. These grooves spur us to take action in such a way as to seem instinctual or unconscious. Once formed, it takes great effort and mindfulness to undo such a groove/habit.

To make changes requires understanding three things: your predominant thought or pattern of thinking on a subject, the emotion associated with the pattern, and the strength/intensity of both the thought and emotion.

Charles Haanel writes in his 1912 book *The Master Key System*:

> *We must 'be' (a state) before we can 'do' (an action), and we can 'do' only to the extent that we 'are,' and what we 'are' depends upon what we 'think.' In other words, your thoughts are creating who you are every moment. Who you are determines your state of being and your state of being stimulates doing.*

Our world is what lies behind our eyes and is colored by filters and interpretations and unconscious bias. It is governed by the mind (conscious and subconscious). When we know this and understand how it works, we can discover the solution for many problems; we can "see" the causes of many effects. Because the world within is subject to our control, all laws of power are also within our capabilities and our creative ability.

At less than a year old, we form impressions based on observations of father, mother, caretakers, and others around us. These impressions form beliefs or unconscious application programs (like the PC's software) that we operate from the rest of our lives. As Jean-François comments in our story, "The sins of the father are visited on the son." This might be a warning of this process, as this is the chain of belief that needs to be broken or dissolved if it is harmful to your well being.

The brain's ability to absorb thought in the formative years from birth to seven is vastly more important than previously thought. What is heard, sensed, or observed about people and circumstances in the immediate environment is all absorbed by our child mind, creating hundreds and hundreds of beliefs without regard for their truth.

Many of our beliefs are ineffective, just not serving our needs, or can be the source of many of our troubles. At ages before our reasoning power could help, we had no ability to judge beliefs as good or bad, helpful or not. The prefrontal lobe, controlling judgment, was still in early development. We had to simply accept what was happening as true.

To see how this plays out for you, examine your beliefs, look at your patterns of action, and ask yourself if they are helping or hindering you. That means asking questions like: What is the belief? Does this belief help me? Where did this belief come from? Is it true? How do I know it is true?

Our minds are much more powerful than we realize. Our limits are self-imposed. We don't believe, for example, that we have any intuitive abilities. Yet, Dr. Russell Targ says in his book *Limitless Mind*, "Most people have the ability to describe and experience events and locations that are blocked from ordinary perception." Beliefs, perception, and experience reinforce each other. Our willingness to examine and question any self-limiting belief is a necessary step in our advancement toward healing past wounds and becoming more of what we truly are, limitless.

Gloria Karpinski, in her book *Where Two Worlds Touch* says:

> *It's not hard to become intellectually facile with concepts, whether they're spiritual, psychological, or scientific. But it's quite another thing to become a living statement of those principles. We long for the truth, discover it, weight it, try it on for size, are confronted with everything within us that it is not, resist the change it demands, and purify ourselves of any remaining dross. At that point there is no more struggle, no more ambivalence. It is who we are.*

Conscious Mind

Psychologists describe the conscious mind as our apparent world because it is self-aware. But what is the conscious mind really and can we see any physiological phenomena related to it?

Electrical engineers have known for more than 100 years that all electrical circuits produce electromagnetic fields. The body, too, has an electrical system and thus has a magnetic field. Some of the most compelling science in this area is from Professor Johnjoe McFadden at the School of Biomedical and Life Sciences at the University of Surrey in the United Kingdom.

McFadden says our conscious mind is an electromagnetic field (he calls this "em"). His theory, according to his website, states:

> *This consciousness electromagnetic information field (cemi field) theory may sound far-fetched, but it rests on just three propositions. The first is that the brain generates its own em field, a fact that is well known and utilised in brain scanning techniques such as EEG. The second is that the brain's em field is indeed the seat of consciousness. This is far harder to prove but there is plenty of evidence that is at least consistent with this hypothesis. Em fields are waves that tend to cancel out when the peaks and troughs from many unsynchronised waves combine. But if neurons fire together, then the peaks and troughs of their em fields will reinforce each other to generate a large disturbance to the overall em field."*

The large disturbance is what he calls "conscious awareness" and what he means by the "cemi—consciousness electromagnetic information—field."

Further research at Paris's Laboratoire de Neurosciences demonstrates the following: if a subject's attention is piqued by a pattern that resembles a face, "synchronous firing in distinct regions of the brain" takes place. If the same subject sees only lines in the pattern, "then his neurons fired randomly." If the subject realized while looking at the pattern that he was looking at a face, "his neurons snapped into step to fire synchronously."

McFadden commented about the lab's work:

> *In this, and many similar experiments, neuron firing alone does not correlate with awareness—but the em field disturbance generated by synchronous firing does. The simplest explanation is that the brain's em field is conscious awareness—the cemi field.*

Let's take an ordinary example. Remember when you learned to drive a car? Remember the fumbling and clumsiness that, over time with constant practice, became automatic actions? Those actions required conscious thought at first, then they became unconscious thoughts, and finally, habitual actions that aren't even in your awareness. This cemi field theory is one of the best explanations of the peculiar features of conscious mind's involvement in the process of learning.

McFadden's research shows neural networks, bundles of nerves, initiating those first uncertain fumblings. The Paris researchers expected these nerve bundles to be in an undecided state during this fumbling, and they were. A small nudge of electrical current, then, from the brain's em field would cause them to move either toward or away from firing. Each time it does this, the em field is "fine tuning" the neuronal pathway (our groove) toward the desired goal.

This fine tuning of a pathway by the em field allows more neurons to connect. Then they fire together and form stronger and deeper connections. The influence of the em field is less necessary with practice, because the activity runs through the prescribed pathways without influence. You drive without consciously thinking about all the parts involved. We call this automatic and at that point it has been relegated to the unconscious mind.

Consciousness

We now arrive at the ground of all mysteries: consciousness. No exploration of mind would be complete without a discussion of consciousness. This is barely a superficial exploration. It would require another book just to examine the many meanings of the word, its origin, concepts, and theories.

Peter Russell, a well-known author and scientist, has a good metaphor for consciousness and how it works.

> A useful analogy is the image from a video projector. The projector shines light onto a screen, modifying the light so as to produce any one of an infinity of images. These images are like the perceptions, sensations, dreams, memories, thoughts, and feelings that we experience—what I call the 'contents of consciousness.' The light itself, without which no images would be possible, corresponds to the faculty of consciousness.

Another scientist in consciousness research, Christian de Quincey, Ph.D., professor of consciousness studies at John F. Kennedy University, says, "… [W]hen we are clear that our use of 'consciousness' means 'primordial interiority' or 'primordial subjectivity,' ambiguity is removed and consciousness and experience may be used interchangeably."

Like de Quincey, David Ray Griffin, author and professor emeritus at the Claremont School of Theology, chooses to define consciousness as experience. Griffin says it is too easy to accept the collective meaning of "self-awareness," preferring the term "experience" as meaning subjectivity.

For our purposes, consciousness is an inner experience. We can describe the universe and our world as "things" or "energy stuff." Physicists have proved that all objects/things are energy, no matter the energy shape. Again, according to de Quincey, "Consciousness is what knows or feels or is aware—of anything. Consciousness is what knows."

Intuition

When someone says they have a "gut feeling" about this, or that they have a "hunch" about something, we classify that as intuition. That is not entirely accurate. Confused? There is plenty of confusion to go around. I believe that what passes for intuition today is actually various functions of the unconscious mind and psychic phenomenon.

It is my idea to link intuition to the more common classification of brain hemispheres. This hemispheric concept of the brain, according to Robert Ornstein, is more than 2,000 years old. He noted:

> *Diocles of Carystus, in the fourth century B.C., saw the two different sides of the brain and their functions much the same way as today's scientists see it. Diocles wrote, 'There are two brains in the head, one which gives understanding, and another which provides sense perception.' That is to say, the one which is lying on the right side is the one that perceives; with the left one, however, we understand.*

In modern times groundbreaking research and neurosurgical procedures began reshaping brain theory. In 1844 Arthur Ladbroke Wigan, M.D., wrote his book *The Duality of the Mind* on the hemispheric functionality of the brain after twenty years of collecting relevant evidence.

Then in 1866 French physician Paul Broca was intrigued with knowing what part of the brain controlled what functions. Through surgery, he was able to find the speech center in the left cerebral hemisphere of the brain—the left frontal lobe—now known as Broca's area. From there Broca began mapping brain functions.

The Russian neuropsychologist Alexander Luria in the years from 1933 to the 1960s performed numerous experiments that contributed to theories of the functional differences between the left and right hemispheres.

By the 1980s, Michael S. Gazzaniga, a neuropsychologist, had been working in the field of cognitive neuroscience. His book *Cognitive Neuroscience III* is an exhaustive look at this subject. He recognized that the brain constantly stores and uses redundant information. Where it stores this information is in question. Some of the higher brain functions such as memory, intelligence, and consciousness, he says, do not have specific anatomical sites associated with their function; instead they appear to be "non-local."

Types of Intuition

I believe some types of intuition can be classified similar to various brain functions. That means we can identify them as:

left-brain function	left-brain intuition
right-brain function	right-brain intuition
whole-brain function	whole-brain intuition
(unknown)	mystical intuition

Note that the first three types are more accurately aligned with unconscious mental processes and the last one, mystical intuition, is what Karl Pribram and David Bohm called part of the "implicate order."

Let's look further at these types, including my definitions.

Left-Brain

> *Left-brain intuition: an unconscious thought process based on experience and knowledge. Characterized by "thoughts that pop in."*

The firemen broke down the front door of the single-floor residential home in Cleveland. They laid their hose lines through the living room and into the kitchen where the flames were shooting all around. The team pointed their nozzles and sprayed the kitchen. The flames continued. They sprayed again, and again the flames continued. The fire lieutenant called his men to retreat to the living room. After standing a moment, he yelled for everyone to get out. As they exited, the floor they were standing on collapsed. They discovered later the fire was in the basement.

The fire lieutenant didn't know why he ordered everyone out of the house. He credited his successful call to "ESP." Gary Klein, Ph.D., in his book *Sources of Power—How People Make Decisions* reported, however, that he didn't settle for this answer and continued to interview the lieutenant about his decision. Several key elements of the story eventually emerged.

The lieutenant said the fire didn't "behave as it should," Klein wrote. The lieutenant said that kitchen fires were supposed to respond to water. This one didn't. He told Klein that he always kept his earflaps up so he could get a sense of how hot the fire was, and he was surprised. This fire was very hot. Finally, the lieutenant said the fire wasn't noisy, and with a fire that hot there is a lot of noise.

This is a perfect example of what I call left-brain intuition. The ability of the unconscious mind to make all the right connections using heuristics (rule of thumb) and deliver the answer in a burst comes as a result of years of experience. In talking about this type of intuition, Klein said, it "depends on the use of experience to recognize key patterns that indicate the dynamics of a situation."

The lieutenant didn't know what to expect because the process was unconscious before he ordered his men out. In retrospect, the clues were there all the time. The fire didn't respond to the water as it should have. The lieutenant didn't know there was a basement. The heat was rising from the basement to the living room and was more intense than it should have been for a kitchen fire. It was quieter than it should have been because the floor muffled the sound. The fire didn't meet the experienced expectations of the lieutenant, and he became uncomfortable. Yet, nothing was conscious except the command to leave the house.

Dr. Russell Targ says in *Limitless Mind:*

> *I believe that intuition comprises the sum total of everything one has learned or experienced in the course of one's life and stored in one's subconscious [unconscious] mind; this background then works together with information that comes to one physically.*

The work of Theodore Sarbin in the 1960s at the University of California at Santa Cruz suggests that left-brain intuition is a "cognitive inference," meaning an unconscious mental process. For example, you might pick up a variety of cues from the nonverbal activities of a person. Their body language, breathing, inflection, and tone of voice might all give you clues from which you can make inferences. All of these are processed through the unconscious and an answer "pops" into the mind.

Consider a person with rapid breathing, fidgety limbs, dry mouth, and a straining voice—all cues telling you that this person is nervous or anxious. You aren't consciously thinking about these cues, but you "have a sense" that this person is nervous. Your past experience with nervousness has been logged into your unconscious and without conscious thinking, but your unconscious knows. This is considered left-brain intuition.

Albert Einstein, the great mathematician and physicist, used a process that sounds like this kind of intuition. According to his biographer, Einstein would work on a problem as long as he felt was needed. Then he would stop, go lie in an open field, drift into a passive state, then fall asleep. It was during his sleep that the answer would "pop up," as he described it. Perhaps it was during this "sleep" that the unconscious mind processed the databank of information based on Einstein's experience and knowledge and returned with an answer seemingly out of the blue.

This would appear to be a left-brain process of the unconscious mind's ability to retrieve and process data outside of conscious awareness, like the lieutenant's. Highly trained people in any field, like Einstein or our fire lieutenant, develop an "intuition" based on their experience and knowledge in a specific subject. This information resides outside conscious awareness, but when called upon, the unconscious mind uses this collective knowledge to provide the answer, and it appears as if from nowhere.

A close friend of mine, Chuck, predicts the financial markets using left-brain intuition. He wakes up at 3 a.m. and writes down what comes to him about the markets for that coming day. He labels these forecasts his "overnight calls" so his clients don't feel spooked about his using this method to suggest multimillion-dollar trades. He says, "This is not coming from my analysis of the market conditions. It is coming from years of experience." Every experience he's had in the markets, and every piece of knowledge, is factored into the "intuitive hit."

This might explain why novice "intuitive" day-traders are fooled into thinking that trading while "in the zone" (using intuition) means not having to know anything. In fact, many day traders believe their ability to predict the right stock is easy. But statistically, 96 percent of them fail to make money. Chuck's clients are some of the wealthiest companies, hedge funds, and institutional traders in the United States. Intuitive trading and trading in the zone were very popular because they allowed anyone to feel they could do what Chuck does, but statistics don't bear this out. Chuck's zone is actually coming from years of experience and is within the unconscious.

Left-Brain Characteristics

uses logic	detail oriented	facts rule
acknowledges	knows object names	forms strategies
reality based	words and language	past and future
knowledge based	math and science	can comprehend

Left-Brain Intuition Type Quiz

1. Do you find that your "intuition" works best when it comes to your job or profession?
2. Do you know answers to questions without thinking about the question?
3. Can you ask a question of yourself and forget it; later, the answer comes?
4. Do you feel you are in a zone when you work, where the answers seem to just come more smoothly?

If you answered yes to most of these, you are a left-brain intuitive.

Right-Brain

Right-brain intuition: a quantum (not limited to time and space) process offering solutions through feeling, symbols, and images. Characterized by "pictures that pop in."

The Gottman Institute, cofounded by Drs. John and Julie Schwartz Gottman, has two major functions as stated on its website. One is "to apply leading-edge research on marriage in practical, down-to-earth therapy" directly to couples. The second is "to provide state-of-the-art training to mental health professionals and other health care providers" who are "committed to helping couples."

What the Gottmans have been able to do is use pattern recognition to help understand couples' behavior. Their research has shown that even the most difficult, complex relationships and problems have an underlying pattern. Couples can detect facial patterns, unconsciously, and know when the other person's actions, statements, and feelings are not congruent.

The ability of our unconscious to find patterns in situations and behaviors is the domain of the right brain. The right brain, meaning right-brain hemisphere, recognizes patterns, trends, and feelings. The right brain knows objects through size and shape without rationalizing or naming.

In a workshop setting someone in pain will ask me to intuit what is causing it. Although I cannot explain how, I perceive or notice the energy in that particular area of the person's body. Then I simply speak, and what I say has to do directly with why that body part hurts. Sometimes I will see an image stored in that area of the body or an emotion being held. This is right-brain intuition. It deals with patterns and the big picture.

These feelings or hunches are intuition. They don't always make sense. They are not always logical. They often can't even be explained, because the answer is not derived from a process of rational thinking but emerges from the hidden processes of the unconscious brain.

Right-Brain Characteristics

uses feeling	risk taking	imagination rules
"big picture"	the present	symbols and images
fantasy based	believes	presents possibilities
spatial perception	impetuous	knows object functions
can "get it" (i.e. meaning)	philosophy and religion appreciates	

Right-Brain Intuition Type Quiz

1. Do you receive answers in symbols?
2. Do you receive answers in your dreams?
3. Can you detect behavior traits within seconds of meeting someone?
4. Do you know something but can't verbalize it?

If you answered yes to most of these, you are a right-brain intuitive.

Whole-Brain

Whole-brain intuition: combines the quantum process of right-brain intuition with the heuristics of the left-brain intuition. Characterized by "pictures with thoughts that pop in."

The two hemispheres, rational and intuitive, are what Timothy Wilson, M.D., and colleagues call our "dual system." Whole-brain proponents say it is not a left-brain intuition or a right-brain intuition; rather, it is both. This means the halves are in partnership. Pattern recognition and spatial processes of the right brain are added to the left-brain unconscious analysis to get the answer.

In his book *Psychosynthesis,* psychiatrist Roberto Assagioli sheds light on whole-brain intuition being the ability to understand the complete picture and synthesize or integrate all the parts back into a whole. He observed that intuition is:

… synthetic function in the sense that it apprehends the totality of a given situation or psychological reality. It does not work from

the part to the whole—but apprehends a totality directly in its
living existence.

Author, futurist, and psychologist Jean Houston says this type of intuition "is guiding from the larger story to the local one."

Here are some interesting facts about intuition from a study by the Institute for Whole Social Science in Carmel, California (also sponsored by Institute of HeartMath), called "Electrophysiological Evidence of Intuition, Part 2: A System-Wide Process."

... [S]urprisingly, both the heart and brain appear to receive and
respond to intuitive information;
even more surprisingly, there is compelling evidence that the heart
appears to receive intuitive information before the brain. ...

Given that the rational mind can never fully understand intuition, it is all theory. So perhaps the decades-old idea that we have left and right hemispheres of the brain, each with different functions and different intuitive processes, is close. Is it possible that the right hemisphere might be the receiver unit and the left, the analysis and transmitter unit?

People who use both hemispheres of intuition demonstrate the ability to intuit in the area of their expertise (left-brain intuition) and with pattern recognition (right-brain intuition). Whole-brain intuition also exhibits the ability to "know" the larger story, which might come in images or symbols.

Whole-Brain Characteristics

logical, fact-based brain	sequential, detail-oriented brain
conceptual, big-picture brain	interpersonal, kinesthetic brain

Whole-Brain Intuition Type Quiz

1. Are you good at recognizing patterns?
2. Does it feel as if information comes through your intuition and that information is being processed by your rational mind?

3. Do most of your intuitive hits come about regarding
   work or a hobby?
4. Do you have the ability to perceive others' emotions in
   social settings?

If you answered yes to most of these, you are a whole-brain intuitive.

Mystical

Mystical intuition: taps the pre-existing wholeness or implicate
order. Characterized by "a knowing."

Nisargadatta Maharaj grew up in a desperately poor area of India. At fifteen, he left home and moved to Bombay, selling cigarettes on the street to make money to send home to his starving family. At thirty, he followed the advice of his guru and enlightenment took place. From then on, he was a sought-after mystic.

Nisargadatta sits in a small sparsely furnished room above his tiny smoke shop. He has animated exchanges with individuals, much like the discussions of the great mysteries that must have taken place 10,000 years ago. And these same conversations will happen for another 10,000 years. His answers to questions are marked by an explicit knowing and clarity.

Mystics have lived throughout time and have taught us that the power lies within us: Lao-tze in the sixth century B.C., Meister Eckehart in the tenth century A.D., Jalal ad-Din Muhammad Rumi in the eleventh, Ramana Maharshi in the twentieth century, and Amma Sri Karunamayi in this century, to name a very few. Each understood this power.

Although mystics appear to be intuitive at an early age, many Indian yogis go through years of rigorous training and practice to develop their mind abilities, including intuition. In the beginning, these yogis learn sleight of hand and mundane magic; they learn the discipline of mind-magic (mind tricks) and graduate to studies of the true mystical powers of the mind. In their final stage, the mystics go beyond the mind, and intuition is their mode of communication with cosmic consciousness.

Mystical intuition is associated with mystical experience. At this level, there is an "otherworldly feeling." Many researchers, philosophers, and scientists have their own way of describing this intuition. For example, in his book *Re-Incarnation and Immortality* Rudolf Steiner says:

> We gain the power to pass over into objective spiritual reality and the third stage of knowledge begins, that of true Intuition, what I have called 'Intuitive knowledge.' ... Through this knowledge something fresh enters the consciousness of the soul; we now learn how man can live within the will which has become independent of the physical body.

Charles Griffon, in his essay "Intuition: An Essential Element of Mysticism," explores a new definition of the word.

> This word [intuition] was apparently developed in an effort to describe what we would literally call 'in-sight' or 'inner seeing,' which is significantly different from a hunch or gut feeling. ... Even the modern scholarly use of the word is inaccurate, where 'intuition' most frequently describes the expectations one might have or the conclusions one might reach from surface observations.

Dr. James Pottenger addresses his view of intuition in his book *Holographic Psychology* and explains what it can mean for us in our everyday lives. He says:

> [Holographic Psychology] is the awakening of Source awareness that is part of a collective consciousness, both innate and transcendent, within each human being. ... It is a force that is invisible, non-tangible yet can be tapped into in a relaxed state of mind. Geniuses like Mozart, Beethoven, Picasso, Michelangelo, Einstein, and numerous others were capable of tapping this level of intelligence. Many mortals have been capable of experiencing glimpses of this altered state of consciousness and the results have often been reported as out-of body experiences or near-death experiences. During this state our reality is altered as it connects

with a level of consciousness for which we generally have no reference point. As a result of such experiences many people live different lives. In the past, most people would have never shared their experience for fear that they would be branded strange or even insane.

Every person has an innate potential, but not every person is capable of developing their inherent potential to its fullest capacity. We believe that the extent to which we develop our awareness is a spiritual blueprint that is decided by a higher or more intelligent force existing within consciousness that is both immanent and transcendent.

Contemplation is one of the key ingredients to mystical intuition. This method turns the focus inward, allowing consciousness to become aware of itself. Desires and intentions dissolve into the greater consciousness flowing into our conscious mind.

Author J. Deikman, M.D., identifies the basic characteristic of mystical experience as the intuitive perception that we are part of a universe that is a unified whole. William James, Harvard professor of psychology in the early 1900s, remarked that such an experience is accompanied by feelings of awe or reverence. He goes on to say it is felt to be a direct experience of a higher reality that is highly valued.

Ervin Laszlo, in his 2007 book *Science and the Akashic Field—An Integral Theory of Everything,* describes an energy field he calls the Akashic, based on the Sanskrit word *Akasha,* meaning "sky" or "ether." Laszlo says all the information of past, present, and future is essentially located in this field.

In her popular book, *The Field,* Lynne McTaggart writes about the Zero Point Field, the equivalent of Laszlo's Akashic. If true, the very essence of what we believe about how the brain and mind store information is overly simplistic. She says, "If they [Walter Schempp, Ervin Laszlo, Karl Pribram] are correct, our brain is not a storage medium but a receiving mechanism in every sense, and memory is simply a distant cousin of ordinary perception." McTaggart goes on to say that interactions of higher consciousness and the Zero Point Field might account for phenomena such as creativity and intuition.

The concept that a single field of data exists containing all past and present information is not new. In ancient cultures the Egyptian, Mayan, Incas, and Hopi all refer to a single field. The Hopi myth refers to Spider Woman's (Creator) web of creation. In the early 1900s, Nikola Tesla, the maverick genius inventor, wrote in his unpublished paper "Man's Greatest Achievement" that space is filled with an "original medium" he also compared to the Sanskrit Akasha. He suggested this kind of force field becomes matter when prana, cosmic energy, acts on it; it vanishes when prana ceases.

"Spirit is constantly deserting one form for another," says Dr. Ernest Holmes in *Science of Mind.* He goes on to say that space in our Universe is not empty but filled with ether, the same energy that makes up matter.

Today we see corroborating evidence of this in the research on dark energy and dark matter. "The universe is made mostly of dark matter and dark energy," says Saul Perlmutter, leader of the Supernova Cosmology Project at Berkeley Lab, "and we don't know what either of them is."

Is it possible that intuition works unscientifically and irrationally, coming to a person in some way from the postulated "field" or the "ether" or "implicate order"? Does this also imply that a person does nothing consciously but simply becomes a receiver for this information from the field? Mona Lisa Schulz suggests it's possible the brain is both transmitter and receiver. Does this signify that information comes from all around us, and in us, and awaits our awareness of it?

Quantum physicist and author Fritjof Capra spoke about intuition in 1997 to Jeffrey Mishlove on his TV program, *Thinking Allowed.*

> *The fact that modern physics, the manifestation of an extreme specialisation of the rational mind is now making contact with mysticism, the essence of religion and manifestation of an extreme*

specialisation of the intuitive mind, shows very beautifully the
unity and complementary nature of the rational and intuitive
modes of consciousness; of the yang and the yin.

For simple people, such as those in third world countries who are uneducated and not prone to using critical thinking, it's much easier to use their intuition because they experience life as wholeness. They're much more intuitive than their analytical and rational counterparts. The mystical intuition is a nonlinear mode of functioning that experiences everything at once without splitting it into linear chains of cause and effect.

Mystical Intuition Characteristics

implicit	holistic
illumined	consciousness of a transcendent order

Modes of Intuition

Identifying the type of intuition—left-, right-, whole-brain, or mystical—helps us define the unseen processes and understand why we have access to certain kinds of intuition. We each have a dominant type that we use most often, and we each have a dominant way of receiving our intuitive insights.

There are four intuitive modalities, or ways we receive intuitive data.

1. Visual

2. Auditory

3. Sensing

4. Thought/Mental

We use all four modes to a greater or lesser extent. One way of determining your mode is to be aware of your language. "I see" is the hallmark of someone who is a visual. "Sounds right" or "I hear you" is auditory and linguistic. "I have a sense" or "I feel" describes someone who is in the sensing mode. The fourth is thought and indicates someone whose answers come as one or two words out of the blue.

Your eyes also are a strong indicator of your dominant mode. Research has revealed that people who look straight ahead or look up when asked a question are generally visualizing. People who are "listening" in their heads for answers will often have horizontal eye movement, meaning they are hearing a voice. Sensing or feeling is indicated by eye movement that is down and to the right. Those thinking about something in thought mode look down and to the left. This theory is a generalization, but it is another tool you can use to give yourself a clue about your intuitive mode.

Eastern cultures assert we have a physical body and astral body. We are familiar with the physical body and its senses. But few Westerners know about or understand the astral body. When you die, you will drop your physical body and operate out of the astral body.

Again, Eastern mystics know this form also has senses. People who have had near-death experiences also report seeing, hearing, or feeling, yet not in the same manner as in the physical body. Is it also possible that senses in the astral body aid certain levels of intuition? Yes. We are unable to understand what is happening from the physical perspective, but our astral body can pick up additional data and pass it to the mind.

Here are explanations of the various modes and how they are used to channel intuitive insights.

Visual Mode

The visual mode is more common in Western societies. Diane worked in a large public relations company. Her job was writing press releases and other company background papers for her clients, and all of her life she thought of herself as a "wordsmith." In a discussion, she said she wasn't very intuitive. So I asked about her intuitive mode, and she said she always "looked for" intuition to come through words or thought. She was convinced she was an auditory or thought type. It was remarkable to her that she tested as a visual.

Not surprisingly, Diane would see in her mind a piece of paper with writing on it. Then she would transfer what she saw to the paper in front of her while reading it with her mind's eye. She wasn't hearing thoughts she transcribed, which would be mental, but she was seeing the sentences already fully formed.

Quiz
Take this quiz to determine if you are more visual than other modes.
1. Do you see images when you close your eyes?
2. When taken on a guided meditation, do you "see" the trip?
3. If someone says "visualize this," is it easy for you?
4. Do you daydream in movies?

Auditory Mode

In auditory mode, you intuit in terms of sound or language. You use the words "I heard this voice say" and "I was listening for the answer." People refer to answers as having loudness or quietness and/or a timbre (distinct quality). People with this mode hear, for example, if this is the time to act.

Quiz
Take this quiz to determine if you are more auditory than other modes.
1. Do you hear answers as coming from a voice or voices in your head?
2. Do you hear sounds that cue you to knowing?
3. Do you love to listen to music?
4. Do you remember conversations easily?

Sensing Mode

Some people feel a shiver or vibration in their body when an intuitive hit comes in. Perhaps you are able to feel the energy of a room or someone else's energy. This is a sensing or kinesthetic mode of intuition.

The so-called "gut" intuition often expressed in business meetings is also a form of sensing. Sometimes a fear in the stomach and a gut-level hunch get confused. Fear is always part of the instinctive or survival mind and not intuition.

On this level, awakening your intuition requires you to pay attention. When you learn to tune into your sensing nature (intuition), you can detect subtle energy changes. This might help, for example, with a matter of changing jobs or finding a partner.

Those using the sensing mode will often use phrases like "I feel" or "I sense." They might talk about the texture of the feeling, of how rough or smooth it is. They will use words like "grapple," "grope," or "grasp."

Quiz

Take this quiz to determine if you are more sensing than other modes.

1. Do you get chills or shivers when you hear or see something?
2. Do you experience a body feeling, such as a "gut" feeling, about things or situations?
3. When you are asked questions, do you look down and to the right to determine the answer?
4. Do you tend to speak in terms like "I feel" or "I sense this"?

Thought/Mental Mode

In this mode people report hearing their own voice and one or two words that "pop in." Intuitive people with this mode say the words have an "absolute" quality to them. The main characteristic is it's a simple and concise couple of words not a conversation or story.

John, an attorney, told me that when he is working on a contract, a thought pops in that has a "different feeling to it," and he knows it's his intuition. It gives him either a "darker or lighter feeling." He says, "It's always right. I can trust it even though I am not sure why."

Often the mind chatter blocks this mode from being stronger; therefore, it is important to notice the feeling of the thought or voice. Many would agree that they have spent most of their lives paying attention to the chatter and perhaps haven't even heard the voice of intuition.

This mode of intuition requires that you spend time developing the space between your thoughts so you allow it, the intuitive thought, to come in. Thoughts are like freight cars on a long train chugging through the mind. Between each car is a space. Take time every day to sit and contemplate this space between your thoughts. Focus your awareness on the gaps or spaces between cars (thoughts).

Quiz

Take this quiz to determine if you are more thought mode than the others.

1. Do you have thoughts that drop in from "out of the blue" with important information?
2. Do you have thoughts that feel absolute in nature?
3. Do you notice these thoughts come more often when you are quiet?
4. Do you have thoughts that are very succinct, often one or two words?

Barriers to Intuition

It is true that most of us have experienced at least one of the types of intuition. What prevents you from experiencing intuition further or more often? Self-doubt, outer-directed focus, cynicism, and judgment are all ways intuition becomes blocked. Intuition can be ignored because we have thought in the past, "I can't be intuitive" or "Some people are just gifted with intuition."

It is also not necessary to be psychic or meditation practitioners of some religion such as Buddhism, Hinduism, or Zen, as books and movies would have us believe in their portrayals, to find intuition a natural experience. Nonetheless, the majority of people tend to be focused outside of themselves on the world out there, and to them intuition is foreign.

The common complaint today is that we are overwhelmed with the amount of information and stimuli that bombards us every hour of the day. For example, we rise in the morning and brush our teeth, turn on the radio for the weather, and grab a cup of coffee or tea (stimulant) as we rush out to work (listening to news on the car radio). We spend the day with telephones, pagers, cell phones, the Internet, Instant Messaging, and texting. Even after we leave the office, our off-hours and recreation in many cases are filled with stimuli such as online gaming, TV, movies, or website surfing.

Clearly, there is little space for intuition. Today's high-technology Western countries tend to draw our attention and awareness outside of ourselves, and we have lost touch with the concept of turning within. To say that this can be a barrier to intuition is a real understatement.

Is it any wonder that our minds are filled with racing thoughts and chatter? The most frequent comment in my workshops relates to the chattering mind. How can I quiet my mind?

Therefore, we have to start a practice of going within. This means that we need to cultivate more quiet time. Whatever practice you choose, even if it is simply sitting quietly, will help you.

Knowledge is another barrier to intuition. Here a major distinction needs to be made. Knowledge and knowing are not the same. Knowledge is what someone else has experienced, remembered, and passed along in some form. It is only supposition until your own direct experience of it. Knowing comes from direct experience.

Knowledge often keeps you from experiencing intuition, because the noise of the mind always believes it "knows." A computer has knowledge but can never know. It has databanks of information, theory, and premises, and yet, it can never have a direct experience.

Often the more knowledge you have of another person, the greater the sense of separation from them because you are not experiencing them. You are experiencing your interpretation of them through your predefined filters.

Another barrier occurs after your experience of intuition. Your rational mind interprets the insight, spinning it like a political spin doctor. When you filter your intuitive insight through your knowledge base, beliefs, or memories, you are likely going to misunderstand or misinterpret the insight.

Judgment is another barrier to intuition. Judgment is closely related to knowledge in that we interpret something through the data we already have and judge it. We make a determination about the insight—right or wrong, good or bad, desirable or not.

How often do you experience yourself judging during the day?

The intellect is about content. It is about knowledge and gathering knowledge. Thoughts continuously flow through our mind even in the middle of the night. When you wake up, you discover you have been thinking. Your mind doesn't appear to shut off. In fact, many great saints talk about deep sleep as the soul leaving the mind's environment so it might have peace. In other words, the mind doesn't stop in sleep; your soul simply leaves the neighborhood to get peace.

Because your mind is processing thoughts all the time, your intuition has trouble surfacing to consciousness. Part of developing intuition is to learn how to focus on the space, or gaps, between thoughts.

NORMAL OR NATURAL

One of the most far-reaching of the findings related to consciousness has been dubbed 'the self-fulfilling prophecy.' More precisely, it is that our beliefs, conscious and unconscious, create the future in

ways more subtle and more powerful than we ordinarily take into
account.   —Willis Harman

Avoid judging from a right/wrong paradigm. This kind of judgment is damaging to intuition and creativity. Clearly, you might not be able to just shut off this critical voice, but this section might help you. Over the course of my research, I found an intriguing concept that distinguishes between what is normal and what is natural.

What Is Normal?

Normal is consistency. It is a combination of the cultural, community, and parental beliefs superimposed upon our thinking. These thoughts become ingrained as our generally accepted truth. All of these overlays are the beliefs of others, and each is having an impact or influence on our lives.

Cultural experience tells us "normal" does not tolerate variation. It does not permit passion, zeal, or aliveness. The words "average" or "flat" are typical descriptions for normal. Spikes of intensity are considered uncontrollable by normal. Normal is control. Normal is the qualitative appeal to the largest number. Ultimately, normal suffocates what is natural.

Whenever I stop being natural and allow normal to take charge, I do things that are heavy; that is, they feel heavy and flat. Working at a job just for the money is normal for me. I might have to do it to create cash flow to survive, but it is not natural.

Normal is not wrong or right—it works for the masses. Natural is not right or wrong—it works for the individual. Leave the judgment out. Observe your behaviors and thought patterns to see what feels normal and natural for you.

Normal is an outside-in process. We are all educated to believe that we must look outside of ourselves to determine who we are, what our life should be, and what we should have. Society dictates these so that people can live and exist within its boundaries.

Our purpose, relationships, livelihood, even health, are all subject to this concept of normal. Parents, preachers, friends, media, scientists, philosophers—all have opinions they wish to share and have us adopt. As we were growing up, we wanted to believe these people and had no reason not to. Or perhaps we wanted to be loved and be approved of by our family and, therefore, we adopted their beliefs.

When we go through life believing only what others know to be the truth, we might be normal but not natural. We begin to mistrust our own knowing, which means we don't know who we are; rather, we only know what we have been trained to know.

Although other people might have built their beliefs on mistaken information, we, believing in them, build our beliefs on their inaccurate understanding. This can result in being bounced along in the chaotic environment of what others believe we should be, should do, or should have, until one day we question it all.

The concept that there is a power within us, within everyone, that can be trusted and relied on for the truth might seem totally foreign, or it might spark a recognition of this truth. This higher Self or higher Mind can lead us to our natural selves.

The world (what is normal) would have you believe that you cannot trust this inner power. Or the world says only certain people have this capacity, but not you. The truth is that you cannot trust that others know what is best for you. They might know only what is best for the masses or themselves. You need to make your choices consciously from your own inner knowing: the power is within—and all the great and sacred texts have said this same thing!

What Is Natural?

In contrast to what is normal, natural is what you know from within. Being natural is to be you. Naturalness is innate to you. You are born with it. But if you have shut off feeling because of some trauma and have been doing what is normal, then you will have to reawaken your naturalness.

Over the years of facilitating workshops, I have found this work natural for me. I have facilitated groups acting out psychodramas, evaluating classical myths, even writing their own biography in the form of a myth. I also have worked with businesses facilitating creativity and innovation workshops, and I coach people to discover what is natural for them—and all of this gives me more energy and a sense of being alive because it is natural.

What is natural is different for each individual; otherwise, it would be normal. What is natural for you might not be natural for anyone else. Natural is trusting that you have within you a grand design and the ability to know it. You can know who you are, where you are going, and what the future wants for you.

"The Universe itself is a giant hologram, quite literally an image or construct created, at least in part, by the human mind," according to Larry Dossey, M.D. This way of thinking about the universe solves many of the puzzles of the unified field. It maintains that all information is contained in the universe and access to this field is accomplished through intuition.

The big bang theory says everything began from the One. Each part that exploded out of the original is still a part of that original, and it contains the whole within it, since everything is connected. Therefore, the answers to who you are and where you are going are already within you, awaiting your authentic inquiry.

How do you make this inquiry?

The most effective way to answer questions is to ask your intuition. Since the field knows all (Lynn McTaggart's *The Field*), then the answers to all questions are also part of the field. Mystical intuition taps this field.

Twentieth-century author Ernest Holmes said, "There is a power for good in the universe and you can use it!" That power is within you, not outside of you; it is within everyone and can be used for good. Great athletes, writers, musicians, and artists practice and train to perfect their form. The same is true if you want to perfect your intuition: practice, practice, practice.

— Section Three —

How to Use

Your Greatest Gift

When the body functions spontaneously
It is called instinct.
When the soul functions spontaneously
It is called intuition.
They are alike and far away from each other.
Instinct is of the body—gross.
And Intuition is of the soul—subtle.
And between the two is the mind—the expert.
Which can never function spontaneously.
Mind means knowledge.
Knowledge can never be spontaneous.
Instinct is deeper than intellect and intuition
Is higher than intellect.
Both instinct and intuition are beyond intellect,
And both are good.
—OSHO

Power of Intuition

You don't have to be a Mystic or Yogi to experience and use intuition. You already have the potential. The everyday mystics, according to authors Clarissa Pinkola Estés, Ph.D., and Caroline Myss, Ph.D., are those living their lives in partnership with divinity or Higher Self, using intuition as a guide. Sometimes, even when people are unconscious of this ability, it might manifest.

George Soros might be called a mystic. He is one of the most powerful modern-day investors, amassing billions of dollars using his own unique insight. Soros's son commented on his father's ability to know the markets and understand when to shift positions in Malcolm Gladwell's book *Blink*.

> *My father will sit down and give you theories to explain why he does this or that. But I remember seeing it as a kid and thinking, at least half of this is bull. I mean, you know the reason he changes his position on the market or whatever is because his back starts killing him. He literally goes into a spasm, and it's this early warning sign.*

Soros is not considered a spiritual mystic in the tradition of Meister Eckehart or Rumi, but an everyday mystic in his ability to use the power of his left-brain intuition, the unconscious voice of experience that comes to Soros through his back.

Gladwell cites another example of everyday intuition in *Blink*. Brian Grazer, a Hollywood producer, met Tom Hanks in 1983, when Hanks was an unknown actor.

> *He came in and read for the movie* Splash, *and right there, in the moment, I can tell you just what I saw. We read hundreds of people for that part, and other people were funnier than him. But they weren't as likable.*

He went on to explain his reasons for wanting Hanks for the part. He concluded, "All this wasn't thought out in words at the time. It was an intuitive conclusion that only later I could deconstruct."

How did George Soros or Brian Grazer learn to use their intuition? Most likely they learned over time to trust this "something" that told them—or gave them a back spasm. It wasn't a conscious process but clearly a learned one. This means anyone can learn to use his or her intuition.

Laura Day, in her book *Practical Intuition,* says, "You develop your intuition by applying it consciously through practice, not by reading about it. Reading is primarily an intellectual act, and your thinking mind can interfere with your intuitive mind." This means use it or lose it! Reading about intuition is not enough: practice, practice and practice.

Terri Collins, of Maryland Heights, Missouri, commented once to me:

> *I didn't realize I had intuition until I participated in your workshop. One exercise was to notice and write down when we didn't listen to our intuition. I did it every day after that. I would keep a piece of paper with me, and I would jot down notes every time I said to myself or another person, 'I should have listened to myself.' I was shocked by the amount of entries on the paper! Sometimes it was only two, but often it was more like eight entries a day. This small exercise changed the way I lived my life. I began listening to my intuition. As the trust grew, I started consciously using my intuition and it was a natural flow.*

There are many people who recognize and use their intuitive powers. A

Google search of "intuition" or" intuitive" yields millions of hits and gives a hint to both the popularity of the subject and the numbers of people claiming intuitive insights.

I explain to people who study with me about the various myths surrounding intuition such as: it's a woman's gift, it's witchcraft, a gut reaction, or psychic trick, etc. The most prominent (but false) concept about intuition is that some people have it, and others don't. In their book *Creativity in Business*, Michael Ray and Rochelle Meyers wrote about business professionals, doctors, lawyers, journalists, teachers, and CEOs using intuition as a guide.

This section is about consciously practicing. I will introduce a variety of exercises for you to practice using your intuition. The processes from the short story can all be found at the end of this section, starting on page 144. For all exercises, it might be helpful to record the exercises using a recorder, have a friend work with you, or download the exercise Podcasts at the website *www.thesecretofknowing.com.*

FIVE STEPS TO INTUITION

Although I have been teaching people for years to use their intuitive powers, it wasn't until I decided to write this book that I systematized the process. But this, like everything, is made up, so try the process and make it your own—and if it doesn't work, try a different way.

What follows are the steps I use to enhance the practice of intuition: Allowing, Attention, Trusting, Asking, and Evaluating.

Step One: Allowing

This step, "Allowing," is about giving your unconscious mind permission to receive intuitive insights. Giving yourself permission might seem like a silly thing, but your conscious and unconscious minds combine to create a filtering system that blocks unwanted, strange, or poorly understood thoughts or processes. Thus, they can stall your intuitive growth. Bringing the conscious and unconscious into alignment by asking your unconscious mind to allow your intuitive insights to come through is a great starting point.

In all these exercises, let any conscious thoughts move through your mind like clouds in the sky—let them travel through.

EXERCISE—ALLOWING

Find a place where you can sit comfortably, uninterrupted, and relax, but not where you will sleep.

- With your eyes closed, take a deep breath and focus your awareness on your feet. Notice any tension in your feet.

- Consciously relax any tense spots by focusing on that area and saying to yourself "relax." Your muscles will begin to loosen up.

- Focus your awareness on your calf muscles and do the same as you did for your feet.

- Continue this until you reach your head. Once you are at the top of your head, allow your awareness to wash over your whole body, back to your feet.

- Give yourself permission to receive your intuitive insight. Say, "Thank you, unconscious mind, for all you do to assist me in living. Please allow my intuition to also support me in any way it chooses."

- Follow your breath. If your attention has moved to a thought and has started building a chain of similar thoughts, move it back to your breath.

- As you notice your mind slowing down, bring your awareness to the gap between the thoughts.

- Don't try to force this process. Just allow it.

Step Two: Attention

Once you have set the stage through allowing, the next step is "Paying Attention," or directing and maintaining your awareness. This is a semi-automatic process for most people. For example, when you look up from reading a book and concentrate your attention on the TV or focus your hearing on the TV, you are directing your awareness. Sometimes you do this intentionally and other times it just happens.

When you meditate, thoughts continue to stream through. At one moment you are chanting a mantra, and at some point, you notice you are thinking about something else. Your mind has attached itself to one thought then built a skyscraper of thoughts about it. When your awareness moves to one of the thoughts then catches another, it is your awareness that is shifting.

One of the gatekeepers of your unconscious mind is awareness. For that reason, what you pay attention to is essential. In the 1950s, ads on radio or especially TV could be used to program your unconscious mind to accept one brand over another. The research psychologist, and one of the fathers of contemporary behavioral psychology, J. B. Watson, helped pioneer the Madison Avenue concept of mind control as it related to purchasing habits. When you walk into your supermarket, you choose one brand over the other without thinking about it. Why? Watson knew! He helped you make that selection. You can change that. Instead of letting your unconscious mind make decisions, use your intuition to make decisions. In this case, let your intuition determine if the item you are selecting is good for you and/or your family.

We know that external data are absorbed through the senses, travel our nervous system, then are transmitted to the brain. The quickest neuropath route for this data is learned by the mind/body and ultimately becomes what is known as a person's "learning style." Learning styles are a way of getting hold of and understanding the world around us.

Your learning style is also the most likely pathway of your intuition. So paying attention to your learning style will help you with your intuition. Are you a visual learner? That is, do you learn quickly from seeing something? If so, your intuition is likely to be visual and you will "see" your intuitive insight through your imagination. Maybe you learn best through hearing, through someone explaining something to you. Or perhaps you are kinesthetic and learn best through sensing and feeling objects. If your learning style is thought/mental, you will be best served to focus your awareness on the silence or gap between thoughts.

The four modes of intuition discussed in Section Two correspond to these learning styles. Remember, they are:

1. Visual
2. Auditory
3. Sensing
4. Thought

Your dominant mode of intuition can be identified through your learning style. The exercises that follow are designed to help you know your style, and that style, in turn, is used to accelerate your learning. At this point I want to assist you in finding your intuitive mode.

Your Intuitive Mode

The following exercises will be helpful in determining what intuitive modality is strongest for you. If your learning style is auditory, the exercises should be recorded and played back (or downloaded from *www.thesecretofknowing .com*). If you are more visual, draw a representation of each step, and while you are going through these steps, use the drawing to accelerate your learning. You might be more tactile or kinesthetic; if that's the case, you will want to find items you can associate with each step. For thought/mental mode, focus on silence.

EXERCISE—FIND YOUR INTUITIVE MODE I

Try this experiment. When you are sitting quietly, notice what you do.

- If you are seeing in your mind's eye or visualizing an upcoming event, going to work, etc., that's the visual mode of intuition.

- If you are hearing a voice in your head talking about an upcoming meeting or some future or past event, that's auditory mode.

- If you are perceiving energy or experiencing a feeling (including energy), that's sensing mode.

- If memories are running in your head about the past or you're having thoughts about the future, that's thought mode.

Begin keeping track in a journal how often information comes through a particular mode: visual, auditory, sensing, or thought. After several days of journaling, you will notice a pattern pointing to your mode.

EXERCISE—FINDING YOUR INTUITIVE MODE II

Find a place where you will not be interrupted. You will need about thirty minutes for this exercise.

- Begin by taking several deep breaths and allow yourself to relax.

- Allow any thoughts to float through and keep your awareness on your breath for about ten inhalations and exhalations, breathing normally.

- With your eyes closed, imagine you are walking from the street into your favorite busy restaurant. You walk in. What do you notice first as you enter?

- Do you hear the sounds of the dishes rattling, waiters clanking glasses, people talking, and the music playing in the background?

- You're led through the restaurant to your table.

  Do you see the colorful and neatly arranged food on people's plates as you pass by?

  Do you smell those wonderful aromas drifting through the restaurant? The newly opened grill creates a wonderful bouquet.

- What do you see around you as you walk through the restaurant?

- What color are the walls? What artwork is hanging and where? What are people wearing?

- Perhaps you notice a person sitting alone at the bar and feel his or her loneliness. Maybe you feel the anger of the waiter as he cancels another order.

- Do you feel the energy of this room? Are people anxious or eager to eat?

- After a wonderful dinner, the waiter comes over to your table and asks if you would like to try the lemon tart. He says they squeeze fresh lemons around the dessert at the table.

- When he arrives with the tart, he has a bowl of bright yellow fresh lemons, and he begins to grate the zest from the peel. As you watch, you realize how wonderful this will be on the tart.

- He asks you to pick a lemon from the bowl. You reach over and pick up one or two and feel the texture.

- He cuts the lemon in half and asks you to taste it to see if you like it. You pick up the lemon half and raise it to your nose and smell it. Then you put it to your lips and begin to taste it. Notice what it does to your mouth and saliva.

- After the wonderful dessert, you leave the restaurant for a walk along the river. What do you notice?

- Take a moment to review and write down everything you noticed.

At what point did you begin to visualize the process? Were you able to notice any physical response to smelling or eating the lemon? Perhaps you felt or thought about the experiment. Or you might have had a combination of these modalities.

If you are a visual learner, you will see in your mind's eye the movie as it happened. You will notice the details of the place: the color, texture, signs, art, what people are wearing, etc.

If you are auditory, the clattering dishes, the rumble of people talking, and the music in the background drew your attention. You noticed the conversations of people at the tables as you passed by.

Did you smell and/or taste the food? Then you're sensory-oriented and even your mouth will water during the exercise. Later you might recall the scene that triggered each sense reaction.

Did you notice thoughts popping up while walking through? That would indicate thought mode.

How you responded gives you clues to your learning style and intuitive mode. Use your specific mode to begin practicing focusing your attention.

Distractions

The mind creates many distractions during intuitive practices, as you might have experienced during the exercises. Isn't it startling all the thoughts the mind allows when you want it simply to be quiet? We all have some form of committee of inner voices distracting us. The mind is like an undisciplined but innocent child with no boundaries, attracted to everything, wanting everything. Mind chatter shows up as thoughts of judgment, jealousy, fear, lack, or constant nagging, desires, expectations, etc. With all these voices wanting attention, is it any wonder you become confused about intuition?

In a meditation group at our spiritual center in St. Louis, first-timers are always interested in stopping the mind chatter, the voice or voices in their head. They are tired of it. For more than 90 percent of humanity, thoughts are continuously moving through their heads like a Texas cattle drive. Where you focus your attention is a choice. Do you focus on the driver, a single stray cow, the dust, the herd, or the grassy meadow you think you see ahead?

To help you determine the difference between mind chatter and intuition, become aware of the energy of these chattering thoughts (cattle). This energy has been described as heavy, chaotic, noisy, pesky, or busy. Intuitive energy is light, peaceful, and certain.

Your mind normally has this cattle drive going on. Your attention might focus on one particular thought because you have an interest, belief, desire, or need that draws your attention to this thought. Once your mind is pulled, another related thought happens. Then another and another, and soon you have a story. If your awareness is tuned into how you receive intuitive insights, you will be able to notice the insights in the gaps between all these thoughts.

Step Three: Trusting

"Trusting" your intuition means you know what to expect. You know how your intuition works for you. Trust is the ability to predict. Trusting your intuition comes as your ability to distinguish the energy of your thoughts from intuition improves. Then you can predict that it will be there when you need it. Some insights into trust:

Trust implies risk.

Trust grows; it does not just appear.

Trust is rational and emotional.

Trust without risk is not possible. Trust must have risk to be what it is. If there is no fear, there is also no risk and no need for trust. How does fear play into this equation? Fear is the result of something you don't understand and feel might harm you in some way. Fear is both thought- and feeling-based. This is true because we stand in the rational mind thinking about possible negative consequences of trusting and the emotional feelings of danger—the result of not knowing what to expect.

Distractions can affect your ability to be intuitive. When you are tired or ill, it is hard to calm the mind chatter long enough to hear your inner voice and focus your energy on healing. This might be true especially when you are first starting to practice. Health is important. When your mental chatter is constant, it is hard to notice your intuition.

Spending time discerning the differences between mind and intuition is consequential. Remember: practice, practice, practice!

EXERCISE—TRUSTING/NOTICING

Use this exercise to help sharpen your intuitive skills and build trust.

- Sit quietly and bring your awareness to the space between your thoughts as you did in the allowing exercise on page 112.

- You have a thought stream going on all the time. Between each thought is a space, a small one at first. As you focus your awareness on the space, it will begin to increase.

- As you begin, the mind begins an endless stream of thoughts, almost in defiance of your goal. Don't struggle with it. Let the thoughts just come and go and keep bringing your awareness back to the space between them.

- One of the first signs along the way to listening to your inner guidance is the feeling of inner peace. This peace is very solid and has a deep sense of connection.

- A sure sign that you are listening to mind chatter is a feeling of anxiousness or blocked, heavy energy. Another sign is when you hear a story, or there seem to be multiple answers to the same question—you are listening to mind chatter.

- Look for the feeling of peace when you are asking questions of your inner self. Also, a sense of flow is the natural awareness of inner self. Answers flow. The feelings flow. There is no sense of being blocked.

Step Four: Asking

Questions and answers are inextricably linked, so asking your question in a way it can be answered clearly and understandably is essential.

Complex questions often result in convoluted answers, and they usually indicate confusion about the subject. A simple question will yield better results. As a novice, I found complex questions didn't work for me, because I seemed to get multiple answers.

A friend will occasionally ask me for an intuitive insight into something that is going on in his life. If he is particularly anxious about something, he will frame the question in complex and mixed ways, such as, "Will I be happy with this new employee?" This question is ambiguous. Happy could mean that he is joyful with this person, yet the person might not do good work. On the other hand, he might be happy with this person's work, yet he or she is a loner. Sometimes splitting the questions helps. Will this employee perform well in this job? Then you can ask a second question. "Will this employee work well together with others?

Here are examples of ambiguous questions.

Will I be happy?

How long before I find the perfect relationship?

These examples show how certain words have multiple meanings and are subjective in nature. "Happy" and "perfect" are subjective. The question, How long before I find the perfect relationship? begs the question of what is perfection in a relationship? Someone who doesn't snore? A person with great eyes? Someone who has good humor? What does "perfect" mean?

Questions need to be worded in such a way that they can be clearly answered. You want a clear, concise answer, so you have to make the question clear, concise, and simple. Otherwise, the answer might come back framed in some way that doesn't make sense.

Furthermore, clients often ask one question that is really three or four questions such as, Will I become richer and happier when I have this new job? Or, If I move, will I find a new smart and young partner who will love dancing? Single-subject, clearly stated questions are best. Will I have ten thousand dollars by May 1st? Will I have someone I enjoy being with by July 4th?

Words have power, and some are loaded with pre-existing baggage. For example, the word "should" can skew your question, as in, Should I take this job? In itself it might just mean, "I am supposed to." But most of the time "should" has parental connotations of undue influence.

Be careful how you phrase things. What is wrong with this question: Since I have never had a car, and have been told I am not a good driver, do you think I can get a car? This is a surefire way to get an answer filled with pre-existing judgments from your left brain (like the question).

EXERCISE—POSING QUESTIONS

The following exercise will help you gain experience in formulating your questions. Write down a question you want answered.

- Write out five ways you can ask the same question, for example, about health.

_____

_____

_____

_____

_____

- Look at your five questions and compare them to the following criteria. Ask yourself if it is:

concise	simple
specific	unambiguous

- Which one of the five ways you wrote the question meets the four criteria the best? Use that one or combine one of them to get the best.

EXERCISE—CLARIFYING YOUR QUESTIONS

This exercise, as well as the previous one, can be used to develop your asking ability. The I Ching, a Chinese divination tool, suggests asking your question twelve times and placing emphasis on different words each time to help clarify it.

Write out your question again, and this time place the emphasis on the first word. The second time you write your question, place the emphasis on the second word; repeat until you have emphasized each word in your question. If you have fewer than twelve words in the question, reemphasize different combinations of words. For example:

> **Will** I be rich next week?
> Will **I** be rich next week?
> Will I **be** rich next week?
> Will I be **rich** next week?
> Will I be rich **next** week?
> Will I be rich next **week**?
> **Will I** be rich next week?
> Will I **be rich** next week?
> Will I be rich **next week**?
> **Will I be** rich next week?
> Will I be **rich next week**?
> **Will I be rich** next week?

Words have energy, and each time you ask the question with different emphasis, the energy will subtly reveal the desire behind the question and point to needed changes in the wording. For example, it might help for you to clarify what "rich" means to you. Is "rich" or "wealthy" the word you really want? Perhaps you will want to specify your meaning and ask again.

Step Five: Evaluating

The ordinary mind is always judging. It is the nature of the mind. By setting some guidelines for interpreting your intuitive information, you can avoid some of the pitfalls of judging. The criteria below can help you assess your intuitive answers.

EXERCISE—EVALUATING TECHNIQUE

The Bible says "the truth will set you free," and Buddha said the truth will "lighten" you up. Using these two statements, evaluate what you receive.

- When you receive an answer, notice: does it feel light and free?

- Become aware of how you feel. Is your energy light? Or is it heavy? If it is heavy, most likely the answer you received came from your ordinary mind. If you sense contraction in your body, again, the answer is most likely from your ordinary mind. If the answer feels expansive and light, you are on track.

Light or heavy is just one way to evaluate intuition. Psychologist Daniel Kahneman, in his 2002 Nobel Prize lecture, said:

> ... [O]ur behind the scenes, intuitive mind is fast, automatic, effortless, associative, and implicit (not available for introspection) and often emotionally charged. Our conscious (explicit) mind is deliberate, sequential and rational, and it requires effort to employ.

Based on this statement, we can say the hallmarks of intuition are:

1. Simple—not a story
2. Rapid
3. Absolute
4. Might defy logic.

EXERCISE—BECOMING AWARE OF INTERPRETING

This exercise helps clarify further differences between how intuition and ordinary mind work. Remember, your intuition might be right, but your interpretation might be wrong. For this exercise, you will need a partner.

- Decide who will be Person A and who will be Person B.

- Stand together face to face with some space between you and the other person, maybe three feet.

- Set a timer for two minutes. Each round ends at the end of two minutes.

- Person A begins speaking first. Let's say you are Person A. When you start speaking, you should not stop but keep talking until the timer goes off. You can talk about anything: what you hear, see, feel, taste, imagine, or think about the other person, the environment, or anything.

- At the end of the two minutes, Person B's job is to repeat back what A said. B should take two minutes and repeat everything he or she heard from Person A.

- After Person B has repeated back to you, compare what you said to what B repeated. You can then switch places and repeat the process.

- Did you notice in this experiment how much interpreting you did instead of simply reporting what your partner said to you? This is how your mind works. Instead of reporting exactly what you heard from your intuition, your mind subtly judges or interprets the intuition. Awareness of how and why you interpret or judge answers is key to not clouding your own intuition. In other words, take the raw information and write it down. Then evaluate it. As you gain experience, you will develop the ability to be non-judgmental about the data you receive.

Summarizing the five steps, they are:

> Step One: Allowing—Give yourself permission to receive intuitive insights.
>
> Step Two: Attention—Pay attention to the way you receive intuitive insights: visually, auditory, sensing, or thought/mental.
>
> Step Three: Trusting—You are intuitive! Trust what you receive.
>
> Step Four: Asking—Ask simple, concise, and specific questions.
>
> Step Five: Evaluating—Was the answer simple, rapid, light, and absolute?

MEDICAL INTUITION

> *I'm saying that we should trust our intuition. I believe that the principles of universal evolution are revealed to us through our intuition. And I think that if we combine our intuition and our reason, we can respond in an evolutionary sound way to our problems. ...*   —Jonas Salk, discoverer of the polio vaccine
> *TIME* magazine, March 29, 1954

Using intuition to determine possible health issues is new for medical doctors, but for the healing arts it is quite old. In more recent history Edgar Cayce, 1877–1943, gave more than 14,000 readings in his life. Best known for his prophecies and past-life readings, he was also known for his distance healings, with more than 9,000 cases for which he diagnosed and suggested various treatments.

Before Cayce, there was another healer, Phineas Parkhurst Quimby. From 1847 until his passing in 1886, Quimby's life was all about healing the sick. In 1859, he opened an office in Portland, Maine, treating more than 12,000 patients by the time of his death. Most notable of those he treated were Warren Felt Evans, a practitioner and author of several mental healing books; Julius and Annetta (Seabury) Dresser, early organizers of New Thought; and Mary M. Patterson (Mary Baker Eddy), of the Christian Science movement.

Today Judith Orloff, Norman Shealy, Christiane Northrup, and Mona Lisa Schulz, all medical doctors, incorporate intuition into their practices. Over the last twenty-five years, lay people such as Carolyn Myss started performing medical readings alongside doctors. Now that has expanded.

Carolyn Myss, in her book *Anatomy of the Spirit,* says:

> As has always happened for me, just when I came to the end of my strength, a new door opened. In February 1992 I was teaching a workshop. … I began the afternoon session by sitting down next to a woman and asking her, 'What can I do for you today?' And she said, 'I don't know. You tell me. I paid my money …' and then it hit me. 'I will no longer do any personal health evaluations on anyone. Instead, I will teach you to evaluate yourselves.'

The result has been a wonderful parade of people, books, DVDs, and schools teaching the practice of energy medicine. This practice in the West incorporates Eastern mystical traditions, such as the Indian chakra energy centers. Myss and Mona Lisa Schulz pioneered their use here, but now they are used by alternative healers and thousands of individuals.

The chakras are areas that correlate to the major nerve junctions of the body. By scanning these chakras with awareness, the organs associated with each chakra can reveal through intuition a person's health issues that need to be investigated. Pain in the body usually indicates a negative belief or thought/feeling. By paying attention to the pain and allowing the pain to inform you, you will be able to avoid chronic health problems.

As we saw, the body has its own intelligence, called instinct. It knows when to beat the heart, clear the throat, eat, and change positions. It knows how to cure a scratch, cut, irritation, or sore. It doesn't know how to communicate in language to the conscious mind, so it resorts to pain.

In my own work I use intuition to sense where a client's body is in pain. Sometimes I hear where the pain is located; other times I feel it. In some cases I see a darkness or color in an area of the body. I might see red in the stomach, for example. Once I receive the information, I then ask the client to "ask the pain what you need to know." In most cases, the answer comes to them. If they have not been ignoring the pain for a long time, the pain usually leaves quickly. In some cases, they have waited so long the pain has become pathological and needs more work, either physical or mental healing.

Often chronic pain is masking hidden beliefs stored in the body's energy field. Once we have identified the specific area of the pain, I ask the participants to focus their awareness there. When I suggest that they ask the pain what they need to know, they usually look at me as if I am crazy. When they do actually focus their awareness on the pain and ask it what they need to know, however, they are almost always surprised by the accuracy of the answer. This answer often deals with a hidden belief the person had been acting on without being aware of it. This can be so frightening that some people block the answer and are not willing to look at it, so they say nothing came up.

As an example, during a workshop a woman in the audience raised her hand to say she had chronic pain in her back. I sensed the energy in a particular spot in her back and asked her, "What's your lower back, right side, saying to you?" She looked shocked. Then she reluctantly proceeded. She stammered, "I feel like I am being stabbed in the back, and there is this image of a car accident I was in twenty years ago." She began sobbing.

She continued, "A thought that popped in just before the accident was 'suicide.' I didn't want to live anymore." Tears were streaming down her cheeks. "I had this thought a split second before the accident." I prompted her, "And … ?"

"I am responsible for the accident and my friend dying," she said through the sobbing.

I asked her if she knew if this was true. She shook her head no. I asked again, "Then why assume you were responsible? It could simply be that your grief wanted an answer and the mind made one up: that you were the cause because of your suicide thought a moment before."

She stopped crying and perked up some. I said, "Has the pain left after all these years of telling that story?" "No," came her reply. I continued, "Ask the pain in your back what it wants to tell you, paying attention to the specific area where the pain is located."

She closed her eyes and said, "What do I need to know?"

"I lost a friend," was the immediate answer.

Then she took a breath and said her back no longer hurt.

The truth was she had lost her friend, but it wasn't her thought that caused it. And it was her story that kept the grief stuck in her back. I saw her at several events over the next few years, and her back has been fine ever since.

In another workshop a young man sat with his right leg crossed over his left. Demonstrating how we lodge beliefs in our body, I asked him what was going on in his right knee. He became nervous and said that nothing was going on. I continued to ask him in a way that made him comfortable, and he finally said that he had twisted his knee three weeks prior.

I suggested that he listen for a message from his knee. He still couldn't come up with anything, so I asked him if he was worried about the future. He replied that he had lost his job the day he twisted his knee. That's when I had him ask the pain for the second time, "What is the belief in my knee?"

His reply was, "There's no future for you." I asked him if that was really true and when he said no, the pain went away, and two weeks later he found a great job.

Beliefs are stored in the body's field. When a belief is causing pain in your body, it is usually a strong indicator of potential trouble in your organs. This kind of disrupted energy can be found in any location within the body. The longer the energy remains, the more the nerve structure tries to signal the conscious mind, using the pain. These types of bodily responses are a source of powerful information about what is going on in your body and what needs to change in your life.

Many of us face health challenges from poor diet, stress, not enough physical exercise, too much weight, or chronic pain. Then we judge ourselves for not getting well fast enough. Thought is cause. Never challenging the validity of our thoughts means strong thoughts with feeling will create, desired or not. Without challenging a thought, we build a story out of it, and out of the story we build, a belief system is created that can be stored in the body.

It might be hard for some people to believe that the body stores memories and beliefs. I remember it was for me many years ago until I read books by Dr. Wilhelm Reich (published in the 1940s). He called it "body armoring" and said that when a trauma takes place, the body stores sights, sounds, smells, and even thoughts in muscles and tissues of the body. I was surprised to learn that the body retains the traumatic experience until it is resolved.

This concept shows up in ancient mythology, dating to the early Greek and Roman periods. Mona Lisa Schulz writes in *Awakening Intuition* that Antiochus, Galen of Pergamum, and *The Decameron* all alluded to the mind/body connection and body memories.

Pain can be a symptom of a belief that is no longer serving you, such as a childhood belief about not being enough or worry about a career change. Sometimes it might be that you are out of integrity with your own moral compass. There could be some trauma that has lingered in the recesses of the unconscious mind and needs healing and surfaces through pain. Using intuition, you can ask the pain what you need to know and release it.

EXERCISE—THE MEDICAL INTUITION PROCESS

This exercise will help you use the medical intuition process, as Jean-François did in the short story to determine what was wrong with the rebel.

- If you have pain in your body, take a moment to sit quietly.

- Take a deep breath and relax. The key to any inner-directed awareness is relaxation. Allow yourself to relax and bring your awareness inside.

- After a few minutes of relaxation, bring your awareness back to your breath.

- After a few more minutes, begin scanning, using your awareness, from the tip of your toes to the very top of your head.

- Notice any heavy energy or dark energy in any areas.

- When you find an area with this type of energy, ask your intuition, "What do I need to know?"

- When you receive an answer:

  Feel the energy. It should feel light and freeing. Make a mental note of the answer and the energy of the answer.

Write the answer down and use the "Guide to Intuitive Healing" below to help you evaluate the answer.

Clear the energy of this area by setting your intention to understand what you need to know and allow the body to release. If the energies still feel dark or heavy, ask your intuition again what you need to know and repeat feeling the energy and clearing it by imagining you're flooding the area with white light.

GUIDE TO INTUITIVE HEALING

This guide to the chakras incorporates work from Mona Lisa Schulz, Carolyn Myss, and Judith Orloff. All have done extensive work in intuition, chakras, and energy healing, and I highly recommend reading their books.

First Chakra

Location: base of the spine

Includes: bones, joints, lower spine

When you scan your (or the client's) body:

- Look, listen, feel, or sense any dark or heavy energy around or above the noted area.
- Stop and focus on the area that has the disruption and ask: "What do I need to know?"

- Listen for words or feelings that bubble up around the theme "lack of support."

Emotional/Mental issues related to this area might be:

a sense of loss	abandonment
dependence	helpless or hopeless feelings
mistrust	superstitions

Potential body issues: chronic lower back pain, immune disorders, personality disorders, addictions, obsessive-compulsive disorders

Other: In this area, pain often indicates a feeling of not being supported and/or not supporting oneself.

Second Chakra

Location: navel, lower abdomen

Includes: reproductive organs, prostate, bladder, large intestines, lower back, pelvis

When you scan your (or the client's) body:

- Look, listen, feel, or sense any dark or heavy energy around or above the noted area.
- Stop and focus on the area that has the disruption and ask: "What do I need to know?"
- Pay attention to anything that feels like limited "personal power." Also listen for words coming from your intuition that relate to "personal power."

Emotional/Mental issues related to this area might be:

fear/insecurity	relationships
finances	production

Potential body issues: lower back pain, pelvic pain, urinary trouble, prostate, ovaries

Other: Collectively, these areas have a theme about creation, creating, producing, and/or "control."

Third Chakra

Location: solar plexus, just above the navel

Includes: abdomen, stomach, small intestines, mouth, liver, gallbladder, middle spine, kidneys, spleen

When you scan your (or the client's) body:

- Look, listen, feel, or sense any dark or heavy energy around or above the noted area.
- Stop and focus on the area that has the disruption and ask: "What do I need to know?"

Emotional/Mental issues related to this area might be:

low self-esteem	concern about appearances
lack of responsibility	overly ambitious
addiction	intimidation

Potential body issues: ulcers, hernias, mouth ulcers, liver, middle back pain

Other: This area relates to self-esteem and personality development and is about responsibility and creating healthy boundaries for oneself.

Fourth Chakra

Location: the center of the chest

Includes: heart, circulatory system (vessels, etc.), lungs, breasts, diaphragm, shoulders, arms

When you scan your (or the client's) body:

- Look, listen, feel, or sense any dark or heavy energy around or above the noted area.
- Stop and focus on the area that has the disruption and ask: "What do I need to know?"

Emotional/Mental issues related to this area might be:

anger	intimacy
forgiveness	nurturing
grief	depression

Potential body issues: asthma, bronchitis, breast cancer, circulation issues, congestive heart failure, heart conditions, shoulder pains

Other: This area has the theme of "emotional balance." Look at your life and circumstances. Is your emotional life in balance?

Fifth Chakra

Location: throat area

Includes: neck, thyroid, teeth, gums, throat, esophagus

When you scan your (or the client's) body:

- Look, listen, feel, or sense any dark or heavy energy around or above the noted area.
- Stop and focus on the area that has the disruption and ask: "What do I need to know?"
- Notice anything related to "personal will" and "divine will."

Emotional/Mental issues related to this area might be:

> inability to communicate needs and wants
>
> inability to listen   loss of will
>
> difficulty making decisions   inability to follow one's dream

Potential body issues: chronic sore throat, gum disease, swollen glands

Other: This area deals with the emotions and connections.

Sixth Chakra

Location: third eye

Includes: brain, eyes, ears, nose, mouth, nervous system

When you scan your (or the client's) body:

- Look, listen, feel, or sense any dark or heavy energy around or above the noted area.
- Stop and focus on the area that has the disruption and ask: "What do I need to know?"
- Notice anything related to "a search for the truth."

Emotional/ Mental issues related to this area might be:

inadequacy	self-evaluation
truth	inability to learn from mistakes

Potential body issues: brain hemorrhage, blindness, deafness, nervous disturbances, stroke

Other: The theme of this center is sensing and learning from the feedback of the world. The world is our mirror, our feedback, and we learn from outside what is happening inside.

Seventh Chakra

Location: internal systems

Includes: immune system, nervous system, muscle system

When you scan your (or the client's) body:

- Look, listen, feel, or sense any dark or heavy energy around the body.
- Stop and ask: "Which system is being disrupted?"
- Notice anything related to "divine nature."

Emotional/Mental issues related to this area might be:

values conflict	inability to trust the Universe
inability to let go of the past	worries of the future

Potential body issues: depression, energetic disorders, nervous system disorders

Other: This area relates to spirituality and the personal connection to the Divine. Integrity issues between espoused spiritual values and actions show up in this chakra.

EXERCISE—CHAKRA SCANNING

Here is a simple way to use your intuitive healing powers for yourself or others. Use the "Guide to Intuitive Healing" (page 133) to assist you in understanding what you receive.

- Hold the intention for a healing to take place.

- Allow your attention to be drawn to any area on your body or the other person's body that has heavy or dark energy, as mentioned in the Guide.

- Place two fingers on the area where your attention is focused; leave them there until the process is complete.

- Allow your attention to be drawn to any other area where the energy is lighter than the energy of the first area.

- Place two fingers from your other hand at that spot.

- Allow your focus to dissolve into silence.

- Notice any intuitive insights that come to you.

- A change in the area, such as either tightening or loosening, means it's harmonizing and you can continue. Imagine the area bathed in white light. When you notice that the energy under your fingertips feels relaxed, the process is complete.

You or the other person might experience an immediate change, or the result might take time for the body to assimilate. The quantum field of the body is an information field, and information can be conveyed from one area of the body to another to balance and heal disrupted regions.

BUSINESS INTUITION

Whenever I have heavy problems I simply introduce the question to my mind, what the problem is, and, in time, I always get an answer. The answer is always there on time.

—James M. Benham, founder of the Capital
Preservation Fund, in *Creativity in Business*

In 1967, Michael Ray arrived at Stanford University, having earned his doctorate in social psychology. He taught classes in marketing, advertising, and research. By the late seventies, he was outwardly successful and inwardly miserable, according to the Stanford University *Business School Reporter.* At one point, he decided to take an art therapy class; the instructor was Rochelle Myers, a multitalented artist and art therapist. Not long after, they began to develop a new course, "Personal Creativity in Business," the first course of its kind in any major university business school.

One aspect of the course was learning to pay attention to the voice within. "Intuition has always been a powerful mainstay of great businesses, but until fairly recently it has been denied as a business tool in the era of over-dependence on analysis," Ray and Myers wrote in their groundbreaking 1986 book, *Creativity in Business.*

Marina Krakovsky reported the effect the two had on their students in the November 2005 *Stanford Business Reporter* story published on the university's website. She wrote:

> Listening to their inner voice took some alums off the seemingly logical career path. Larry Smith, Sloan '01, says that when Cummins Engine paid his way through the competitive one-year Stanford program, the company viewed him as 'one of the fast-trackers, to be gross about it.' So, when he left Cummins just a couple years later to work in the nonprofit sector—taking a

pay cut of about $40,000—some people said he was crazy. But those who knew him well weren't surprised. Smith, now associate director of the Center for Philanthropy at Indiana University and a lay minister in his church, hasn't looked back.

A lot of creativity and innovation results when people wake up to their inner resources. Students in the Stanford course listened to business executives such as Masaru Ibuka, co-founder and chairman of Japan's Sony Corp. Someone asked, "What is the secret of your success?" He replied that he has a ritual of making an herbal tea and asking, "Should I make this deal or not?" He continued that if the tea gave him indigestion, he wouldn't make the deal. "I trust my gut, and I know how it works," he said. "My mind is not that smart, but my body is."

Akio Morita, Sony's other legendary co-founder, didn't care much for research. It was his belief that no amount of market data could have predicted the Walkman's success. Even his top engineers had serious doubts about his idea for a personal listening device.

The idea that intuition is more common than most people believe comes from a 1994 survey by Jagdish Parikh. He reported the results of a survey where managers were asked if they used intuition. Of the 1,312 managers in nine countries surveyed, almost 80 percent said they use intuition on a regular basis. Equally impressive were the comments on the survey that said that intuition contributed to their corporate success. Many of these same managers defined intuition as "non-logical thinking," "a feeling from within," "a gut feeling," "a sixth sense," or "spontaneous knowing."

Much of business history is brimming over with stories of intuitive decision-making. Some others examples of interest include Jonas Salk, who discovered the polio vaccine; Andrew Carnegie; Nolan Bushnell, founder of Atari games; Paul Cook, founder of Raychem; and Steve Jobs, co-founder of Apple computers.

Many other well-known people have used their intuition for business purposes such as billionaire George Soros and his methods of shifting positions in the financial markets based on his back pain.

Intuition does not recognize any level of individual based on money, intelligence, fame, or any other qualification. It is available to all. For example, Jim Hood, of St. Charles, Missouri, is an information technology consultant and tells this story:

> *I first discovered my intuition while watching the stock market. I began to notice a pattern where I would get strong senses of 'knowing' in my abdomen at times when certain stocks were about to have substantial growth. Sure enough, every time I would get a gut feeling in that area, it was no more than a few weeks until the stock would appreciate dramatically.*
>
> *This same sense of knowing came as I was considering a full-time employment offer in I.T. [information technology] with a company I was working with as a contractor. The sense of knowing was very strong and unambiguous that I needed to accept their offer. Having seen the wisdom of this knowing from my stock market experience, I said yes.*
>
> *Just a few months later, the dot-com crash of 2000–2001 affected the company, and as budgets shrank, the company let go many contractors. Those contractors that remained were required to take a substantial pay cut. Employees, however, were able to weather the downturn unscathed. Had I not honored my intuition, I could easily have found myself in a severe financial situation.*
>
> *Since these experiences, every time I have a sense of knowing in my abdomen and chest, I act on its guidance without hesitation. I am still amazed at how it 'knows.'*

Colin Powell, former secretary of state, said in *My American Journey*:
> *Dig up all the information you can, then go with your instincts. We all have a certain intuition, and the older we get, the more we*

trust it. ... I use my intellect to inform my instinct. Then I use my
instinct to test all this data. 'Hey, instinct, does this sound right?
Does it smell right, feel right, fit right?'

I believe good decision-making is a combination of intuitive and analytical processes. In many cases, as I noted earlier, the type of intuition that relies on what we already know unconsciously is the most frequently used type in business, i.e. left-brain intuition. That is to say, most business executives who have a strong intuitive decision-making ability also have years of experience in their field. When someone of this type makes a snap decision, usually they have digested materials about the potential decision long before the decision arrives.

Best-selling author and business consultant Peter Senge sums up the relationship between reason and intuition in his book *The Fifth Discipline*:

People with high levels of personal mastery do not set out to
integrate reason and intuition. Rather, they achieve it naturally,
as a by-product of their commitment to use all the resources at
their disposal. They cannot afford to choose between reason and
intuition, or head and heart, any more than they would choose to
walk on one leg or see with one eye.

Robert Medearis, founder of Silicon Valley Bank, has a similar philosophy, as quoted in *Creativity in Business*.

... [L]isten to your body, listen to your gut, allow intuition to
come forth. You likely understand what 'gut feeling decisions'
means. They are talking about your subconscious. They are
talking about listening to your body, about letting the energy
inform you. Listen to your intuition and believe it. You have it,
but you've got to learn to believe it.

In the early 1980s, working as a business consultant, I met real estate tycoon and entrepreneur Claude Rosenberg. I was hired to work out some business processes for his RREEF Corporation. He told me he had learned early on that making decisions with his intuition led to his career successes.

What is especially notable about these examples is that the people who had the intuition insights learned to trust them and acted upon them for use in their everyday work lives. Buckminster Fuller once said, "I call intuition cosmic fishing. You feel a nibble, then you've got to hook the fish." As Fuller suggests, it is not enough to have the insight. You also have to have the follow-through by taking action given you in the answer to your question. Perhaps you will need to ask several times before you receive what it is you need to take action on.

The following exercise will help you get started by accessing your own business answers.

Exercise—The Business Answer

- Begin by sitting in a quiet and relatively dark place.

- Close the right nostril with the right thumb and inhale through the left nostril, counting eight heartbeats.

- Now close both nostrils and retain the breath four heartbeats.

- Exhale through the left nostril, counting eight heartbeats.

- Wait for an interval between breaths of four heartbeats.

- After some practice, begin to increase the time of each inhalation to twelve, sixteen, and twenty-four heartbeats, increasing the time of retention, exhalation, and interval of breaths in the given proportions.

- Bring your business question to mind.

- Allow yourself to notice any intuitive thought or feeling.

- If nothing comes up, allow the question to return and repeat the silence.

- When the answer is understood, begin the follow-through.

EXERCISES FROM THE SHORT STORY

There are four exercises Jean-François discovered in the short story. He calls them processes, and I wanted to include them here because I might have stimulated your curiosity in the short story.

As the story noted, the cosmos is in constant motion. The difference in objects, chiefly, is their varying rates of vibratory motion. Everything has a definite rhythm or measured beat. Your rhythmic rate is discovered by learning your pulse beat rhythm. This is to be regarded as your unique rhythmic measure and is to be adhered to in all your practice of rhythmic breathing.

There are several points on the body where your pulse rate can be detected. On the thumb side of the wrist is the most common place to check. At that point, the artery is near the surface, making it easy to find your pulse. It is this spot health practitioners use when taking your pulse.

The practice of intuition does not require breath work, meditation, sitting in one place, getting quiet, or a preset environment. That said, in the beginning stages when you need to focus, a quiet place and a process are helpful. But know that once you understand your dominant mode of receiving and the vibration of your intuition, you can access and use it anywhere and anytime.

Ocean Process

The first exercise helps you center yourself and prepares you for the other exercises. In our short story Jean-François says:

> *'In normal conditions we receive the vibrations and rhythms of the great ocean of life through our intuition, and we respond to them. But in today's world we are so choked with information, hundreds of decisions daily, too much to do, old memories, and such that we fail to receive the impulse from what is called Mother Ocean. Consequently, disharmony and chaos manifest within us and all around us.*
>
> *'This first process ... helps us get in touch with that rhythm again. ... Each pulse beat, or heartbeat, is your rhythm and connects you to the rhythm of Mother Ocean. There is a part on the etching that says, 'One pulse or heartbeat is one unit.' He paused.*
>
> *'Great metaphor, isn't it?' he said.*

EXERCISE ONE
(1 unit = 1 pulse/heartbeat)

- Begin by closing your eyes.

- Close your right nostril with the right thumb and inhale through the left nostril for a count of six units.

- Hold it for three units then exhale for six units.

- Close your left nostril with the left thumb and inhale through the right nostril for a count of six units.

- Hold it for three units then exhale for six units.

- Inhale through both nostrils for a count of six units.

- Close both nostrils and hold your breath for three units.

- Exhale, alternating between your left nostril and right for six units.

- Wait for three units between and repeat this whole cycle three times.

The Gap and Space

The second exercise expands on the process Katie experienced in the story in concentrating on the gap. This process will help you focus your ability to visualize or imagine space in the body, ending with gaps between your thoughts and discovering your inner silence. It is also important in the other exercises. Combining the first and second processes with either of the other two will give you a richer, more rewarding creative experience.

EXERCISE TWO

Sit in a comfortable position or chair with your feet on the floor. Allow twenty to thirty minutes for this to start; expand the time as you become more proficient.

- First, take several deep breaths and allow your body to relax.

- Relax your feet … your calves … knees … thighs …

- Relax your back … hips … shoulders …

- Relax your arms and hands …

- Relax your head … relax your eyes … mouth … neck.

- Feel the energy in your body.

- Imagine the gap between your ears.

- Imagine the gap between your eyes.

- Imagine the gap in your throat.

- Imagine that the gap inside your throat expands and fills your neck. As you inhale, it gets larger … as you exhale it gets smaller.

- Imagine the gap between your shoulders.

- Imagine the space between your ribs.

- Imagine the space inside your lungs.

- Imagine the space between your hips.

- Imagine the space between your knees and your feet.

- Imagine the space between your feet and hips.

- Imagine your chest region totally filled with space.

- Now imagine the gap between cells.

- Imagine the gap between the molecules in your body.

- Imagine the gap between atoms in your body.

- Imagine the space in the universe.

- Gently imagine or visualize the gap between your thoughts for as long as possible.

Creation Process

The third exercise is the Creation Process and is similar to ancient Tibetan rituals.

EXERCISE THREE

Center yourself with the Ocean Process (page 145).

- Begin by closing your eyes.

- Close your right nostril with the right thumb and inhale through the left nostril for a count of six units.

- Hold it for three units then exhale for six units.

- Close your left nostril with the left thumb and inhale through the right nostril for a count of six units.

- Hold it for three units then exhale for six units.

- Inhale through both nostrils for a count of six units.

- Close both your nostrils and hold your breath for a count of three.

- Exhale, alternating between your left nostril and right, for six units.

- Wait for three units between and repeat this whole cycle three times.

- With your awareness, see your vision moving from your mind's eye to your heart.

- Wait twelve units, noticing how it feels and what emotions are coming to you. Intensify and prolong good emotions.

- Use your awareness to move the vision from your heart region to the first chakra at the base of the spine. This is where the image vibrates and attracts the equivalent in matter.

- Wait twelve units, noticing how it feels and what emotions are coming to you. Intensify and prolong good emotions.

- Hold the vision for at least forty-eight pulses or heartbeats. When the vision feels real, you can stop.

Remote Viewing

The remote viewing technique can be used to find objects or to help you look for a new home or see what your children are doing.

EXERCISE FOUR

Center yourself with the Ocean Process (page 145).
Option 1: To find an object or look for something.

- Imagine you are in the vicinity of the object.

- Notice the surroundings and every detail you can about the area.

- Hold this picture for at least forty-eight pulses or heartbeats.

- This may give you clues as to where the object is.

Option 2: To see where your children are playing.
- Imagine or pretend that you are looking out of your child's eyes.
  - Look around and notice what is happening.

- Hold this picture for at least forty-eight pulses or heartbeats.

Conclusion

I started this book with a short story, because I agree with the supposition that people respect non-fiction but read fiction. Therefore, I thought it would be appropriate to include an entertaining story about intuition as a thriller. There is also another reason for the story. Metaphorical or mythical stories operate on the unconscious to open the reader to possibilities. I wanted to open the door to the possibility that we all have and may use this intuitive power.

In Section Two, I chose to review what science is saying and put forth possible explanations that enhance our ability to understand our own experience of intuition. We have heard from experts, mostly scientists, on their views about intuition. I have proposed a way of understanding intuition that, although neither scientific nor scholastic, is aimed at everyday readers looking for a way to grasp their experience of intuition. I purposefully avoided the typical approach to intuition as being associated with angels and non-physical beings, and its possible association with dark angels or sinister characters.

Finally, in Section Three, I presented exercises that can help you rediscover your intuition and practices to help you hone this ability. Because of my own background in medical and business intuition, I chose to briefly cover these topics with more of an eye toward practice than theory.

Bibliography

Assagioli, Roberto. *Psychosynthesis.* New York: Viking (1971)

Bard, Arthur S., M.D., and Mitchell G. Bard, Ph.D., *The Complete Idiot's Guide to Understanding the Brain.* New York: Alpha (2002)

Begley, Sharon. *Train Your Mind, Change Your Brain: How a New Science Reveals Our Extraordinary Potential to Transform Ourselves.* New York: Ballantine Books (2007)

Bohm, David. *Wholeness and The Implicate Order.* London: Routledge (1996)

Capra, Fritjof, Ph.D. *Thinking Allowed.* Thinking Allowed Productions (1997)

Coaster, R. A. "Intuition and Decision Making: Some Empirical Evidence." *Psychological Report,* Vol. 51 (1982)

Day, Laura. *Practical Intuition.* New York: Broadway (1997)

de Quincey, Christian. *Deep Spirit.* The Wisdom Academy Press; *thewisdomacademy.org* (2008)

Dossey, Larry, M.D. *Space, Time and Medicine,* fifth edition. Boston: Shambhala Publications (1982)

Estés, Clarissa Pinkola, Ph.D. *Mother Night: Myths, Stories, and Teachings for Learning to See in the Dark.* Sounds True, Inc. (2009)

Gazzaniga, Michael. S. *The Cognitive Neurosciences III.* Boston: MIT Press. (2004)

Gladwell, Malcolm. *Blink: The Power of Thinking Without Thinking.* New York: Back Bay Books (2007)

Gottman, John M., Ph.D. and Julie Schwartz Gottman, Ph.D. The Gottman Institute. *http://www.gottman.com/* (2009)

Haanel, Charles F. *The Master Key System.* Wilkes-Barre, Pennsylvania: Kallisti Publishing (2000)

Holmes, Ernest. S. *Science of Mind.* Los Angeles: McBride & Sons (1932)

Hothersall, David. *History of Psychology.* New York: McGraw Hill (2003)

Jenkins, W. M., and M. M. Merzenich, M. T. Ochs, T. Allard, and E. Guic-Robles. "Functional Reorganization of Primary Somatosensory Cortex in Adult Owl Monkeys after Behavioral Controlled

Tactile Stimulation." *Journal of Neurophysiology,* Vol. 63, Issue 1 (1990)

Kaku, Michio. *The Physics of the Impossible.* New York: Anchor (2009)

Karpinski, Gloria. *Where Two Worlds Touch: Spiritual Rites of Passage.* New York: Ballantine Books (1990)

Klein, Gary A. *The Sources of Power—How People Make Decisions.* Boston: MIT Press (1999)

Laszlo, Ervin. *Science and the Akashic Field—An Integral Theory of Everything.* Rochester, Vermont: Inner Traditions (2007)

McCraty, R., M. Atkinson, and R. T. Bradley. "Electrophysiological Evidence of Intuition: Part 2. A System-Wide Process." Institute for Whole Social Science and Institute of HeartMath. *The Journal of Alternative and Complementary Medicine,* Vol. 10, No. 2 (2004)

McFadden, Johnjoe. "The Conscious Electromagnetic Field Theory." Surrey, England. www.surrey.ac.uk/qe/cemi.htm. (2009)

McTaggart, Lynne. *The Field: The Quest for the Secret Force of the Universe.* New York: Harper Paperbacks (2008)

Myss, Caroline, Ph.D. *Anatomy of the Spirit: The Seven Stages of Power and Healing.* New York: Three Rivers Press (1997)

New World Encyclopedia. http://www.newworldencyclopedia.org/entry/Paul_Broca (2010)

Orloff, Judith, M.D. *Positive Energy: 10 Extraordinary Prescriptions for Transforming Fatigue, Stress, and Fear into Vibrance, Strength & Love.* Harmony Press (2004)

Ornstein, Robert. *The Evolution of Consciousness: Of Darwin, Freud, and Cranial Fire: The Origins of the Way We Think.* New York: Simon & Schuster (1991)

Parikh, Jagdish. *Intuition: The New Frontier in Management.* London: Wiley-Blackwell (1994)

Pinker, Steven. *How the Mind Works.* New York: W.W. Norton & Company (2009)

Pottenger, James P., Ph.D. *Holographic Psychology: The Science of Spirit.* San Diego: Community Church of Religious Science (2010)

Powell, Colin. *My American Journey.* New York: Ballantine Books (1996)

Pribram, Karl H. *Languages of the Brain: Experimental Paradoxes and Principles of Neuropsychology.* New York: Prentice-Hall (1971)

Ray, Michael and Rochelle Myers. *Creativity in Business.* New York: Broadway Books (2000)

Russell, Peter. "The Primacy of Consciousness." *http://www.peterrussell.com/SP/PrimConsc.php* (2009)

Sarbin, Theodore. *Clinical Inference and Cognitive Theory.* New York: Holt, Rinehart & Winston (1960)

Schulz, Mona Lisa, M.D., Ph.D. *Awakening Intuition: Using Your Mind-Body Network for Insight and Healing.* New York: Three Rivers Press (1999)

Schwartz, Jeffrey M., M.D., and Sharon Begley. *The Mind and the Brain: Neuroplasticity and the Power of Mental Force.* San Francisco: Harper Perennial (2003).

Senge, Peter M. *The Fifth Discipline: The Art and Practice of the Learning Organization.* New York: Broadway Business (2006)

Targ, Russell, Ph.D. *Limitless Mind: A Guide to Remote Viewing and Transformation of Consciousness.* Novato, California: New World Library (2004)

Vaughan, Francis E. *Awakening Your Intuition.* San Francisco: Anchor (1978)

Wigan, Arthur Ladbroke. *A New View of Insanity: The Duality of the Mind.* London: Longman, Brown, Green, and Longmans (1844). Available at google.com/books

Wilson, Timothy, M.D. "A Model of Dual Attitudes." *Psychological Review,* Vol. 107 (2000)

We invite you to continue your experience with
The Secret of Knowing at our website

www.thesecretofknowing.com

Rev. Larry De Rusha has traveled the country
giving lectures and keynote speeches, and
facilitating workshops.

His Secret of Knowing workshops are dramatic—
Larry becomes the character Jean-François
from the short story and brings life
to the science and exercises!

For workshop or lecture information,
please contact us at 314-576-6772.
Or email
revlarry@earthlink.net

10975537R00100

Made in the USA
Charleston, SC
21 January 2012